Beyond Humanism

Beyond Humanism

Towards a Philosophy of Catholic Education

by

JOHN JULIAN RYAN

SHEED and WARD
New York, 1950

To my Mother

Contents

Acknowledgments

For permission to use much of the material which appears in this book, I wish to express my gratitude to the following: Dr. Roy J. Deferrari, General Director of the Catholic University Workshops; Very Reverend Monsignor Frederick G. Hochwalt, Secretary General of the National Catholic Educational Association; Rev. Michael J. McKeough, Editor of *The Catholic Educational Review*; Rev. Francis P. Moran, Editor of *The Pilot*; and Mr. Vincent J. Giese, Editor of *Concord*.

The Author

I

Secularism

THERE are few Catholic educators today who are so smug as to believe that the institutions which they conduct are perfect. Rather, they feel impelled not only to make a careful examination of conscience, a full confession, and a firm resolution never to sin again, but also to work out a clear-cut way of life and a method for following it. They are more than willing to accord a fair hearing to anyone who attempts in any way to diagnose their ills and to prescribe possible remedies for them.

All of which is not, of course, to say that Catholic educators have been derelict or that the education which they have afforded has been of no great value. The truth is that, depending for their necessarily meager funds on a class of people far from well-to-do who were burdened by having to support two school systems, public as well as parochial, and surrounded by bigotry, snobbery, and Philistinism, Catholic educators have, by their devotion and toil, literally wrought wonders.

Furthermore, any Catholic school, by its very nature and by the character of those who conduct it, can hardly fail to afford an education that is essentially profound—one that normally should be more profound, on many counts, than that provided by a similar non-Catholic institution. For, at the very least, a Catholic school is a place where the student will find Christians; a place where he can be sure of breathing the air of Charity; a place where he will find instructors most of whom are trying to be saints and some of whom are saints; a place where he will find some much-loved person ready to help him at all times—guiding, consoling, inspiring, in a Christian intimacy of master and disciple far surpassing any that is commonly maintained in non-Catholic institutions. Above all, the Catholic school or college, its hearth an altar, is a spiritual home where the student may feel himself to be one of the household of God, cleansed, guided, animated by Our Lord Himself.

It is with a full appreciation of these facts, then, that I venture to call attention to the secularism by which Catholic education has become infected and from which it must rid itself.

For, whatever our feelings may be in acknowledging them, the symptoms do seem to bear out the diagnosis that our institutions have become unduly secularized. In students, in teachers, in textbooks, even in class-rooms, our institutions, especially our colleges, differ altogether too little from those conducted by non-Catholics.

To consider the students first, since it is by the quality of its fruit that a tree is to be judged primarily: unless I am greatly mistaken, if you ask most undergraduates in Catholic colleges what their reasons were, or even what their reasons ought to have been, for coming to college, they will give you an answer that is hardly very reassuring. Half the reasons they present will be vaguely Christian; the other half will be clearly un-Christian. They will tell you glibly that they have come to St. Swithin's to make sure of a thorough grounding in Catholic principles, or to become Christian gentlemen who will be leaders in their community—all fairly straight out of the catalogue. But if you go on to ask them why they are taking the courses that they are taking, rather than any other set—why they are specializing, for instance, in Chemistry or Physics or Economics or Biology or Education or the Classics—they will betray how dismally little their Catholicism has to do with any of these. The reasons they commonly give you for taking such courses are, at worst, those of an agnostic and a go-getter; at best, those of a Deistic humanitarian. They will tell you that they have to be realistic; that they are living in a world of "dog-eat-dog" competition in which, unless they are armed with the same knowledge and understanding of things as that possessed by their opponents, they will not be able to fight their way up to the top. Of course, while a fellow is making his pile, as well as after he has made it, he ought to be able to enjoy most of the higher things of life: he ought to be able to follow with some understanding the latest developments of science, appreciate a good book or a good speech, even cultivate a taste for poetry. Every well-educated man ought to be able to carry on an interesting conversation no matter what the topic; he ought to be able to talk about something besides the latest movies, the articles of the latest *Reader's Digest*, and cartoons in *The New Yorker*. After all, there is something more to life than sports and business.

As for anything like an enthusiastic interest in religion—in Theology or the Liturgy, or even the Encyclicals on social matters—well, how many articles on these subjects appear in our Catholic college magazines; how expertly are they written; how widely and enthusiastically are they read—especially as against, let us say, the articles on football?

And if we observe the graduates of Catholic colleges, we find them hardly less symptomatic of secularization than are the undergraduates. Once having kissed their dear old alma mater good-bye, many of them put her ideals as well as their caps and gowns in mothballs; they preen themselves on their ability to fit into the pagan world; they are afraid that others will not think of them as good Americans and "regular guys"; and they become proud of having got ahead. Nor do they so much as suspect that this "success" is often something of which Our Lord would rather have them be deeply ashamed. They are, in fact, despite their courses in Logic, victims of a fallacy that might well be re-named the diocesan newspaper fallacy; to this effect, that if a man is a great industrialist, and he also happens to be a Catholic, then he is a great Catholic industrialist; or, if he is a great politician, and he also happens to be a Catholic, then he is a great Catholic politician; and so on.

Finally, I somehow think it might prove a little embarrassing to ask Catholic graduates how many books on dogma or the liturgy they had read during the first ten years after graduation.

But if our students are secularized, so too are many of our teachers. They too have fallen prey to the fallacy just cited; they have come to believe that if a man is a great scholar or a great teacher, and he is also a Catholic, he is a great Catholic scholar or teacher. Some of them, it would seem, are anxious to preserve the purity of their disciplines at all costs—even at the cost of letting the students shift for themselves and draw unsound and heretical conclusions from what they have learned. Especially is this statement true of teachers in those fields in which students need most desperately to correlate their scientific thinking with their philosophic and religious—fields like Chemistry, Physics, and Biology. Sometimes these men have no other training than that of a purely secular, positivistic and agnostic college, so that they simply do not know that there is such a thing as a Cosmology to which their science is subordinate—to say nothing of an Ontology or a Theology. And what is true of the teachers of the physical sciences is true also of the teachers of the social sciences: it is shocking, for example, to find these latter capable of giving courses in Economics, Politics, Sociology, and History, without so much as without troubling to correct their course and re-orient themselves by the light of the Star of Bethlehem.

But whatever the excuse, the fact remains that too many of our teachers are professional men who happen to be Catholics; too few are Catholics who happen to be professional men.

Not the least cogent evidence of the secularization of our institutions is afforded by the textbooks we are content to use; and I am referring here not only to those written by pagans for pagans, but also to those written by Catholics for Catholics. To cite but one or two examples of those that I can recall having seen in use: there was the Physics Laboratory Manual introduced by a quotation from Huxley to the effect that only the measurable is true and worthy of investigation; there was the introduction to Poetry which did not even mention the poetry of the Bible; there was the book of Epistemology that omitted all reference to the Spirit of Truth; there was the book of Apologetics which gave the impression that one could reason his way, entirely unaided, into the Faith; there were the Psychology textbooks (Dynamic as well as Speculative) which dealt with man as an animal with an intellect rather than as a spirit which can be and needs to be incarnate; books which give the impression that he is a creature with no conscience, for the understanding of whom it is not necessary to know that he is in the image and likeness of God, that he has been harmed by Original Sin, and that the well-spring of his actions is love. Surely textbooks like this cannot be said to be as Catholic as they should be.

Evidence of our secularization is presented, I think, even in our very class-rooms; for there is little in these to suggest that learning is a divine, not merely a human, thing; that the Spirit of Wisdom is also the Spirit of Love; that skill and Charity go hand in hand; that the Truth is beautiful; that

mentioning, to say nothing of defining properly, the do
of Original Sin and its effects.

Perhaps I am being too harsh or judging from too li
an experience; I hope so; but I cannot help thinking that
of the classes in these subjects which I have had any occa
to visit or learn about indirectly have differed from sir
classes in non-Catholic colleges only by being preceded
followed by a prayer. Can most of our teachers of Phys
Chemistry, or Mathematics say that there would be mu
more than the prayers before and after class and the cruc
over the blackboard to indicate to a stranger who had wa
dered into one of their classes that he was not at the Mass
chusetts Institute of Technology or the California Institu
of Technology.[1] Would not many of our teachers of th
courses in Business Administration now being given in ou
(God save the mark!) Liberal Arts colleges feel compli
mented if they were told that their classes were just like those
at the Harvard Graduate School of Business Administration?

The fault here, I hasten to add, is not wholly that of the
teachers; some of the blame for this condition must fall on
the Deans and Administrators. For the teachers are often
encouraged to believe that there is a fundamental and final
cleavage between scientific, philosophic, and religious truth
by noting that the men who get their Ph.D. degrees in no
matter what science from institutions that are thoroughly
secular are paid quite as high a regard as that paid to men
who get them from Catholic institutions. Deans and Administrators not seldom overlook the fact, pointed out by
Aristotle, that once you start on the wrong angle, the further
you go, the further you get from the truth; they seem to believe that scholars, having started on a pagan angle towards
a pagan goal, can somehow end up in the City of God, even

[1] For a further consideration of this point, see Appendix D.

any one class-room is only another meeting place where disciples and master are to learn to love God and fellow-men through studying the wonderfulness of their handiwork, as well as to serve them through acquiring the skills necessary for that purpose. Where are the Physics and Chemistry laboratories decorated with the *Benedicite*; where are the Economics classrooms decorated with scenes of Christ scourging the money-changers in the Temple, or with such inscriptions as *Blessed are the poor in spirit* or *You cannot serve God and mammon?* Do not our class-rooms, like those of our pagan friends, subtly convince students by their antiseptic efficiency that learning is a matter of acquiring, somewhat painfully, under impersonal, dehumanized, puritanical conditions, the letter of the truth, not the spirit—certainly, that it has little to do with enhancing the Gifts and enjoying the Fruits of the Holy Ghost through a study, as it were, of the blue-prints of God the Father and a uniting of self to His Son?

Perhaps I am being meticulous or too severe, but I cannot help wondering what a Buddhist monk of Tibet might think when, after he had visited the class-rooms of Harvard and then those of some of our own institutions, he were told that, as their recent report states, the members of the Harvard Faculty do not believe "that education can be safely left with those who see our culture solely through the eyes of formal religion," whereas we consider education to be essentially religious. Would he not be rightly puzzled?

Now, to understand the secularization evidenced in these various ways, it is necessary for us to realize that it is primarily the result of our efforts to resist heresy and the forces of heresy. In dealing with pitch, we have become contaminated by it. Let me try to diagram briefly the history of this contamination.

It began, according to some, with the advent of the so-called Reformation. For at that time, it became necessary for Catholic Doctors and teachers, in establishing a system of Apologetics, to do three things, all of them somewhat dangerous. First of all, they had to emphasize the external marks of the Church. Second, they had to justify the special position of the clergy. And third, they had to arm the laity with arguments by which to controvert heretics. And these actions, although good enough in themselves, had certain very unhappy consequences.

The emphasizing of the fact that the Church, though a Mystical Body (Protestants, as well as Catholics, granted this) was also an organization, the most important members of which were the clergy, had the very unfortunate effect of making Catholics forget that they were all living members of Christ, all called to "grow up in all things in Him." The regrettable fact is that this emphasis on the external marks of the Church made it easy for Catholics to come to feel that this organization was primarily an *instrument*, something *between* them and Christ, not an extension of Christ Himself into which they were absorbed as living and active parts. They were no longer to live Christ with the help of their lives; they were to live their lives with the help of Christ.

The second of the three apologetic duties, the justifying of the special status in the Church of the clergy, had a similar effect. Men began to feel that since the celebrating of the Mass and the administering of the Sacraments were the work of the clergy, they simply were not the work of the laity. They fell into the habit of passive receptivity, content to be "spectators" who knew less about what was going on before them at Mass than they did when they watched a public execution or a football game.

Finally, the arming of the laity with arguments for the

controverting of heresy tended to confirm the mentality of what Wilfrid Ward has described as "the state of siege." With their teachers feeling that every Catholic, if possible, should have Basic Training in polemics, the laity began to rest more and more content with that training alone. Their attention concentrated more and more on defensive and minimal truths; such as, that Catholic dogmas were, after all, not against reason; that one's main need was simply not to fall into heresy; and that, therefore, one could be a "devout Catholic" and still take little or no interest in Theology or the Liturgy. The time was to come when fewer and fewer of the laity were to be trained in understanding the depth and splendor of the Church or of their privilege in living its Divine Life. Their case in appreciating the Bride of Christ is much like that of a person who is asked to fall in love with a veiled woman by being told that what her enemies say about her is not true.

All these things worked together, then, to produce an almost deadly sloth and spiritual blindness. For, as soon as religion becomes the art of avoiding heresy and grave sin, as soon as a boy can feel sure that the one thing that matters is taken care of for him by the agency of the hierarchy, then it becomes easy for him to assume that all secular activities, being relatively unimportant, amount practically to indifferent acts. If he goes to Mass every Sunday and to Communion every First Friday; if he avoids not only sin, but the occasions of sin, as both of these are commonly understood, then he is "a good Catholic boy" and "a credit to his family, his town, and his parish"—even though, in every other way, he leads so entirely pagan a life that he soon becomes the head of a thoroughly un-Christian corporation or political pressure group or even college.

It would seem, in fact, that a fatherliness that has lapsed

into paternalism has not only accepted this condition as normal, but has actually continued to assure it by providing means for worldly success. Because the clergy wish above all things that Catholic boys should come to them for instruction, so that these boys will not lose their souls through ignorance of Apologetics or lack of spiritual guidance, they accede to the demands of parents who want their sons to get ahead in the world. The clergy thus permit the teaching not only of dangerously secular subjects (like Money and Banking) without putting these under the supervision of a moral theologian, but also of general physical science for its purely positivistic or commercial value. "Love God, and then do what you will" has been translated into, "Study Religion, and then take any course you want."

In other words, to assure that their students will have as good a chance to get ahead as other boys, to satisfy parents who want their sons to have what they themselves never had, Catholic teachers who reject violently the religious teachings of heretics accept willingly their scientific and philosophic teachings—often, indeed, trying to outplay the secularists at their own game. They do so despite the history of secular education which, having fallen under the influence of a relatively mild form of Epicureanism, has ended in a luxury-loving pragmatism. The history of the last four hundred years has shown that men who give up hope of attaining the Beatific Vision with the help of God try to regain an equivalent Paradise here on earth by relying entirely on their own powers. Feeling that they will never possess the joys of eternity, they concentrate on assuring the comforts and delights of time, mastering sciences in order to change Nature into a source of comfort and of thrills or in order to enjoy the glamor of its mysterious principles and mechanism.

The attempt to live by these ideas was, of course, foredoomed for many reasons, not the least of which was that in trying to attain an impossible certitude—the certitude of angels—so as to enjoy the highest of intellectual pleasures, men found their minds so inadequate that they came at last to doubt the very powers of reason and to rely on purely sensory and emotional—one might almost say neural—tests for truth, goodness, and beauty: a theory was true only if it worked; and it worked only to the extent to which it provided new gadgets, or satisfied the ache of curiosity, or provided a new aesthetic thrill. The artist began to be esteemed because, being super-sensitive, he could provide others with intense imaginative and intellectual titillation; the scientist, because he enabled inventors to relieve aches and pains, and, presumably, to guarantee increased leisure; the cleric, because he could make us feel religious. Those who prized dedicated craftsmanship and the humble scientific searching out of the blue-prints of God so as to make clear His Glory and so as to enable craftsmen to imitate the operations of Nature, and the unsentimental heroism of saintliness—the men who prized these things came to be less esteemed than the nature-lover, the connoisseur, and the humanitarian—than those, that is, who had an intense *love* of Nature, a *feeling* for animals, a *responsiveness* to new ideas, a *sensitive appreciation* of the Fine Arts, a *love* of efficiency, a *sense* of the Brotherhood of Man, and a *respect* for religion. God Himself is no longer to be worshipped gratefully as the Love Who Created; He is the great cold-blooded Mathematician and Self-Appreciator Who can certainly find in us or in any other fortuitous concourse of atoms nothing that is worthy of His appreciation. The myth of Christianity is, to be sure, a "true myth" in that it is a good restorative to have handy for black moments, ceremonial occasions, and mornings-after; but it is true only for the consolation it affords; for myth it is, after all.

The dominating motives throughout this evolution—or, rather, revolution—being enjoyment through control of Nature and delight in scientific truth for its own sake, two delusions were fostered: first, that the highest education is properly concerned not with arts, but with sciences—a college of liberal arts being, in fact, a college of liberal sciences— since "knowledge is power," and knowing how to do a thing results simply from knowing how it is done; and, second, that skill is to be acquired simply in order to enable its possessor to enjoy luxuries and the pleasures of knowing.

That man, it would appear, is truly well-educated who acquires the kind of information that enables him to get ahead in the world, to bring up a family, to raise the standard of living of his neighbors through affording them better plumbing or cheaper television, to improve the slums by philanthropy, and to spend his leisure time in visiting art museums, enjoying the latest books and plays, the latest symphony, even the latest ballet. He is not, of course, "too religious," but he has a nice appreciation of the fact that religion is a good thing, something which should, so to speak, be kept going: it assures the sanctity of the home; it guarantees against perjury; it safeguards the right of private property; it affirms the dignity of man, which is the basis of Democracy; and it is the bulwark of the State. No one is well-educated who fails either to try to raise our standard of living, so that all may enjoy a "more abundant" life or to realize that in this effort religion can prove a very useful thing.

The college, therefore, in which one is to acquire this kind of information and training is rightly a place of fellowship where one attends lectures, takes notes, memorizes passages of text-books, carries out the mysterious instructions of laboratory manuals, and, in general, tries to get good grades by passing examinations. Through enduring these often seemingly pointless activities together, through attending the meetings of societies and clubs, and through following, with common interest, the fortunes of a football team, one learns what it is to make valuable contacts, to get along with others as a member of society, to enjoy the satisfactions of an *esprit de corps* and the gayety of youthful community life; so that, years later, one can rejoice in memories of "those good old college days."

Now, as I have said, unless I am greatly mistaken, most Catholics would see in this picture nothing wrong, except the failure of the student to go to a Catholic church and to receive some instruction in Apologetics. Many would label as, if not "crack-pot," at least too "idealistic" the alternative view that, in truth, he alone is well-educated who has acquired the wisdom and skill needed for acting as charitably and professionally as possible, the intention and the technique needed for restoring all things in Christ.

II

Clearing the Ground

IF MOST of what I have said thus far is sound, if it is true that
we have become secularized through fighting heresy in religious matters and embracing it in secular matters, what is the
remedy? How are we to go about reconstructing our institutions?

Here we face, if my analysis has been correct, the necessity, first of all, of ridding ourselves of five unfortunate ways
of thinking and then that of revising our institutions accordingly, taking advantage of present circumstances, which, on
the whole, are in our favor.

The five dispositions of which we may well be rid are
these: that of self-complacency; that of human respect; that
of the worship of knowledge (gnosiolatry); that of paternalism; and that of thinking unrealistically.

Certainly, if we are to make any change for the better,
our first act must be one of self-examination. We must make
it a habit to study our deficiencies searchingly—never resting
content with the knowledge that however inadequate these
institutions may be, at least they are better than those which
promulgate heresy. We must give up all practices of flattering
one another and all forms of snobbery.

It would, in fact, be well for us to put aside all com-
parisons and rivalries. We can do with fewer hours spent in
criticizing non-Catholics; we can concentrate a little less on
what they are doing and a little more on what we are doing;
we can make fewer attempts, born not seldom of the un-

acknowledged feeling of inferiority, to outplay the agnostic at his own game; we can resist conformism, keeping our eyes less on the grandstand and more on the ball.

Particularly, let us not imitate our pagan friends in the outright worship of knowledge, in their unhappy prizing of curiosity. For, if curiosity can kill a cat, it can also kill a Catholic. It can seduce him into believing such harmful notions as that there is no such thing as mental gluttony; that any knowledge, since it is immaterial, must be spiritual and therefore a good in itself; that there are no ways of evaluating truths except as primary or secondary, basic or derivative, and hence that, all knowledge being a good in itself, any scholarly investigation of any topic is a good in itself; that an educational institution which is devoted primarily to the turning out of Catholics must become anti-intellectual and pragmatic unless it fosters in its students an intense intellectual curiosity —the passionate desire for knowledge as an end in itself, the passionate love of knowledge for itself alone. Worst of all, curiosity can confirm learned Catholics, even learned Thomists, in the belief that no other position on these matters is even conceivable. Apparently the fact that intellectual curiosity is a sin—at times even a mortal sin—seems to have been noted by few modern Catholic educators and by only one Thomist—St. Thomas himself. And since the only way of dealing with this question which would satisfy most modern Catholic educators or most Thomists is to do the very un-Thomistic thing of using an argument from authority, it may be well to note carefully what St. Thomas has to say on this subject.

The citing of his doctrine on curiosity may help here since it implies that all schools should primarily be concerned with one aim: that of developing habits of studiousness rather than of curiosity.

For, St. Thomas himself, with his usual skill in making vital distinctions, saw clearly that studiousness is one thing and curiosity is another, and that they are not to be confused. Studiousness is the enthusiastic ("vehementem") application of the mind in acquiring the *right kind* and the right *amount of truth*; curiosity is the enthusiastic application of the mind in acquiring indiscriminately *any kind* of truth in *any amount.* Studiousness is a virtue; curiosity is a vice.

And odd as it may seem to moderns, St. Thomas did not distinguish between these two habits on the basis of the quality of the knowledge acquired—on the immateriality, the abstractness, or the profundity of it. St. Thomas considers it as bad to gulp down purely intellectual knowledge as it is to gulp down any other kind. As a philosopher, he sees clearly the value of intellectual study; as a saint, he sees just as clearly its subtle dangers. That the truth is good in itself; that the appetite for acquiring the truth is good; that the exercise of the faculties in satisfying that appetite is natural and good: all this, as a sound Aristotelian, he is happy to affirm. But he does not permit his natural enthusiasm to sway his judgment here; he speaks out distinctly and powerfully against all forms of mental intemperance. He points out that intellectual curiosity can be harmful in several different ways.

First, of all, once a student has acquired intellectual knowledge (and the merit badge or the Phi Beta Kappa key that goes with it) he may find it a twofold source of temptation: he may let it make him conceited; or he may find himself using it to commit still graver sins.

For, as St. Thomas points out: "The appetite or zeal ('studium') for knowing the truth can be directed either towards or away from its right object. And, in a way, it is peculiarly true that the more a person comes by a knowledge of the truth, the more he lays himself open incidentally to evil: consider those who apply themselves to acquiring a knowledge of the truth so as to be able to lord it over others. It is for this reason that St. Augustine says: 'There are those who, disregarding the virtues, and not knowing what God is and how great is the majesty of Nature as it maintains an ever-unvarying course in its action, think they are doing something big when they devote to this huge bulk of matter we call the earth a study as intense and as curious as possible. As a consequence, so great grows their pride that they come to think of themselves as inhabiting that very heaven about which they are always wrangling.' "

The temptation of using intellectual knowledge for sinful purposes seemed so obvious to St. Thomas that he gives it only a sentence or so: "Those also who strive to learn something for a sinful purpose are indulging in study that is vicious, as Jeremias says (IX, 5): '. . . . they have taught their tongue to speak lies; they have labored to commit iniquity.' "

St. Thomas then goes to four other ways in which intellectual curiosity can be vicious, his remarks on one or two of these being enough, I should think, to make some of us teachers blush a little.

The first of these ways is that of acquiring knowledge which, literally, is none of our business. On this point, St. Thomas says flatly that intellectual curiosity is vicious "to the extent to which a study of things that are not very useful holds people back from a study of those things which they are obliged to study of necessity." In other words, men are to be judged, first of all, by whether they know what they need to know for their vocation and their salvation—not by whether they are persons of broad general culture. It is one thing to star on *Information Please*; it is another to be wise. St. Thomas makes this point quite clear by quoting for his clerical audience a statement of St. Jerome's: "It would seem that we priests, having put aside the Evangelists and the prophets, spend our time reading comedies and singing the love-songs of bucolic poetry." And although this was written for fellow clergy, it is hard to believe that St. Thomas would not have been equally strict with lay students who neglected Christ in favor of Culture.

But it is perhaps when he comes to the two last dangers of curiosity (he lists six, all told) that St. Thomas says what is of most importance for educators today.

For a man may sin not only by neglecting divine truth; he may sin also by resting content with secular truth, allowing himself to become enthralled by it. Or, to put this differently, he may not only ignore the two Gifts of the Holy Ghost, Science and Wisdom, but he may also sin by cherishing exclusively the gifts of Eddington and Jeans—or even of Aristotle. Charmed by the mysteriousness of scientific discoveries, he may easily neglect the Mysteries of Revelation. And yet, St. Thomas points out, a man commits a sin when he "desires to know the truth concerning creatures while not keeping in mind the proper end, that is to say, the knowing of God." He utters, in fact, a terrible criticism of our courses in Economics, Physics, Chemistry, Mathematics, and the like, when he goes on to quote from St. Augustine these words: "In the study of creatures, we must not exercise a vain and passing curiosity; but the step from them to the Immortal and the Unchanging must be taken."

Lastly—and this is a point that might well be kept in mind by those whose false sense of democracy causes them to lower standards and nurse along students who have no moral right to a higher education—intellectual curiosity can easily ruin those who dabble in things above their heads. As St. Thomas observes; "it is thus that men fall into errors; for, as Ecclesiasticus (III, 22) says: 'Seek not the things that are too high for thee, and search not into things that are above thy ability; but the things that God hath commanded thee, think on them always, and in many of his works be not curious.' " To which he adds a later verse (26) from the same chapter: "For the suspicion of them"—that is, as the context shows, of the things above their understanding—"hath deceived many, and hath detained their minds in vanity."

All of which does not in the least imply that students are not to be taught the physical sciences; or that they are to be taught only those things that would be of use to an apologist alone; or that when they are studying a science, they should think at all times of its theological implications, never concentrating on it *as if* it were an end in itself. Nor does it mean that the student is to acquire *only* the information that is "of necessity" in his trade or profession.

It simply means that the *first* principles of integration for any course of studies should be those of Charity (the love of God for His Own sake and of neighbor out of love for God) and skill.

St. Thomas's treatment of curiosity and studiousness suggests, in fact, a very useful check-list of questions like the following:— Are we, by our prize competitions, our appeals to self-respect, or our flattery, encouraging the acquisition of intellectual knowledge (worst of all, of a "good grade") with no regard to the fact that it "puffs up"? Do we, in teaching Economics, Physics, Chemistry, or what not, try to make sure that the information we are imparting will not be used simply "to get ahead in the world"—ambitiously, enviously, uncharitably? Are our students more learned in the words of God than they are in the words of men? Do we always hand them a kind of Jacob's ladder whereby they may take the step from a knowledge of creatures to a knowledge of God? Do we encourage students to dabble in things far above their capacities, turning them into complacent wise-fools, irredeemably vague, shallow, and glib? Is our every institution of learning, in short, worthy of the name given to its medieval prototype, the name *studium*: a place of zeal? Or is it just another Old Curiosity Shop?

Now, when we have rid ourselves of respect for mere curiosity, we must next, it seems to me, rid ourselves of paternalism. May we have done, once and for all, with coddling —with the feeling that the student is, after all, "just a boy." May we make our standards as high, not as average, as possible. May we rid ourselves of the "we'd-better-take-them-and-keep-them-here-or-they-will-go-to-a-non-Catholic-college" motive, and try to make at least a good number of our institutions famous as places very hard to get into and very hard to stay in.

For, the college which does set goals of achievement as *high as possible* is the college which guarantees not only to its own exceptionally gifted students the training they deserve, but also, indirectly, to the less gifted students of other colleges as high a training as they can take. As everyone knows who has followed sports, unless an athlete aims at what seems an impossible record, he is not likely to do as well as he can; and once a record has been broken, almost every athlete can equal or come near to equalling it. And so for the spiritual athlete: it is only by aiming at profound spirituality and great technical skill, that he makes new records in education; and once he has made these, an astonishing number of his fellows, even of the faint-hearted, will approach, if they do not equal, his attainments.

Nor will the college itself suffer. For the first few years, it might; but as soon as it got known for what it was, it would be flooded with applications. Institutions may die of mediocrity; they thrive on excellence. Sensible boys want the best; so do sensible parents.

Unless we eliminate coddling, we shall, in fact, run a risk far greater than at first meets the eye. For, the high school senior who, in looking about for a college, sees that a very stupid friend of his gets good grades in a Catholic college and another of better endowment gets only average grades in a non-Catholic college, is not likely by that observation to be prejudiced in favor of the Catholic college, but against it. The good-hearted, paternalistic dean who accepts the dim-witted student thereby unconsciously drives away the brilliant student. And this same brilliant student, losing his faith, becomes in later life a positive and devilish enemy of Catholicism. Maybe the City of God benefits by that kind of thing; but maybe not; and I beg of our administrators to consider that it may not. *If only for the sake of the weak, we must also be just to the strong.*

Finally, we must rid ourselves of bookishness and become once more realistic—in the sense in which a saint is realistic. Under the influence of the Gifts of the Holy Ghost (and what could be more realistic than relying on the Spirit of Truth and Love?) we must learn to judge everything we do or say, all our discipline and teaching, by a Christian taste for the real; we must shape all our instruction with such points as these in mind:—

(1) That God is the Reality of reality itself;

(2) That the only life really worth living is that of knowing, loving, and serving Him in this life and enjoying Him in the next;

(3) That real men are primarily creatures in the image and likeness of God, but harmed by Original Sin;

(4) That we have been given the privilege, in trying to live the only life really worth living, of becoming one with God's own Son as a member

of His Mystical Body, so that we can live, in some sense, His Very Life throughout every year, every day, every minute.

(5) That we have been given the privilege of restoring all things, especially the things of civilization, in Christ, acquiring and applying our skills in a spirit of Charity;

(6) That, in so doing, we must come to know our fellow-men and all other creatures both as individuals and as members of the real cosmos, which includes not only the earth, but hell, purgatory, and Heaven.

(7) That in all this our greatest single enemy, our real enemy, is a proud *Spirit* called Satan: a *Spirit*, not a brute, whose main opportunity has been man's lust for experience, and whose primal and present weapon is curiosity;

(8) That, although ideas are real, they are meant primarily to serve as lenses, enabling us to see the reality of things; hence, they are not so much to be sought and enjoyed for their own sakes as they are to be sought for the focussing of our minds on whole things, that we may not only see these, but may see into them to their nature and through them as specimens of His infinite wisdom and love, to God Himself;

(9) That any education is therefore unrealistic, disintegrative, and diabolical which trains a student to study and formulate the appearances of things as if these appearances had no substantial basis, unity or meaning, and as if the principles governing them were the true and final objects of study, all whole substances being merely mysterious, accidental combinations of these

principles, not really meant, not *historically* meant, by God; that any education, indeed, is tragic which trains him for living only one side of life, the animal, and concentrates his attention on living intensely only certain parts of life (the moments of highest sentimental pleasure, however intellectual) merely coercing him into living as cooperatively as he can without losing his individuality; for nothing could be more unreal than training one part of the student—the faculties needed for scientific investigation and voluptuous enjoyment—to deal with one section of Nature, one set of aspects at a time, in order to live a life as a wilful part of the cosmos, and to enjoy, even so, only those parts of his existence in which he is thrilling most intensely to one isolated experience;

(10) That every Catholic student is, on the contrary, to be trained realistically to lead a whole life, as a personal part of the whole Body of Christ, being thus a coadjutor of God in restoring the whole of humanity, of civilization, and of nature in Christ; that he must deal with wholes, hence cultivate above all his cogitative sense[1] (which was given to him for that purpose) under the guidance of his intellect and under the influence of a will responding to the Gifts of the Holy Ghost; thus being trained in the truly liberal arts, those which free us from sin and error, even from the sin and error of prizing them too highly and of enjoying them for their own sakes.

[1] For a fuller description of the nature and work of the cogitative sense, see Chapters 9 and 10.

It is incumbent upon us, then, to keep in mind at all times the fact that man, created in the image and likeness of One Who is Pure Act and Love, as well as Wisdom, is meant to learn, first of all, how to keep in fullest action—that is, how to act most givingly. This statement means that he must know *how* to act, not merely know the precepts of Charity; and he must know how to act as efficiently as possible, so as to act as charitably as possible—not merely know the requirements of efficiency. In short, he must be trained in technical and spiritual skill, the one in the service of the other. He must be given not knowledge for the sake of power, nor information for the sake of success, but scientific skill for the sake of living Christ at all times; he must be given a technique under the guidance of Wisdom, Understanding, Counsel, Fortitude, Knowledge, Piety, and Fear of the Lord.

To this end, our system of education must again become realistic and practical in the true sense of these words: neither merely intellectual, on the one hand, nor merely utilitarian, on the other. Without neglect of speculation, we must again give wisdom precedence over knowledge, performance over memorizing. The long-misprized cogitative sense must again be seen as the faculty on which the teacher must center his efforts. Above all, our students must be trained carefully and profoundly in the spiritual arts required for living Christ, especially in the arts required for active participation in the public worship of the Church.[2]

---

[2] "Therefore it is necessary, Venerable Brothers, that all Christians consider their principal duty and highest dignity that of taking part in the Eucharistic Sacrifice; and this not with a passive and indifferent spirit, or distracted and wandering to other things, but so profoundly and so actively as to be most intimately united to the great High Priest, according to the word of the Apostle: 'Have this mind in you which was also in Christ Jesus'; making this offering together with Him and through Him, and together with Him sanctifying themselves." (*Encyclical on the Sacred Liturgy*, the *Mediator Dei.*)

The task of reforming our institutions in accordance with the principles I have tried to indicate here will not, I know, prove easy. In a country fascinated by the glamor of Epicureanism, it will be hard indeed for educators to tell students and parents that education is concerned with self-denial more than with self-indulgence, with self-abnegation more than with self-expression, with great sanctity more than with great success, with the Gifts of the Spirit of Wisdom and Love more than with the latest discoveries of agnostics, with a hidden life in Christ more than with prominence. Against such educators will be environmental forces of all kinds: advertisements which insinuate that ease and enjoyment are the ends of life and that success is the highest goal; newspapers, magazines, radio programs, lectures which all imply that to be what they call well-read and well-informed is to be well-educated; novels, moving-pictures, stage plays, which in a thousand crude and subtle ways suggest the desirability of pagan living and hence the desirability of an education which fosters pagan living; and, perhaps worst of all, our teachers' colleges and our state and private university rating authorities, who practically make it mandatory for apprentice teachers to absorb at least some of the poison of hedonism, positivism, egalitarianism, and pragmatism.

Unquestionably, all these things are against us; all these forces do hem us in; but there are infinitely greater powers in our favor. Pride and Original Sin work against us; but for us work the Wisdom of God and His Love, especially as these have been manifested of late in the castigation and disciplining of mankind through His providential nemesis. Few indeed have proved so befuddled as not to have been shocked into sober fear by prison camps and atom bombs alike. Even rugged individuals have been stunned into acknowledging the need, if not for Charity, at least for a semblance of it called

III

The Blue-Print

WE HAVE been considering, up to this point, the possibility
of our improving Catholic education through a recognition of
our faults and through an adoption—or a readoption—of certain basic principles. But it is fairly certain that we shall do
little to improve our system of education radically if we limit
ourselves to the taking of such steps as these. We must try,
rather, to get a synoptic view of Catholic education as a whole
and then come down for a careful study of each of its details,
to see what it implies technically.

And to get this synoptic view of Catholic education, we
must, first of all, observe what it is for—see what its place is,
not only in society, but also in the whole cosmos.

That place can best be understood in the light of the
following truths:— The cosmos was brought into being by
God, Who, if I may use the term reverently, is Generosity
Itself: Who is a society of Love: a Father who gives Infinite
Love to a Son Who gives Infinite Love in return, their Mu-
tual Love being the Holy Spirit. This All-Loving God, in an
astounding act of generosity (He suffered no need to do so)
freely called from nothingness into existence a vast and ordered cosmos of creatures, that they might enjoy the privilege
of sharing in His perfections.

One of these creatures, man, He made to His image and
likeness, giving to him the charge and the chivalric honor of
being a co-worker with Him. Man was to have the privilege
of giving himself back wholly to the Father, as well as that

of aiding all other creatures to do so through acting as their voice. He was thus to be priest and prophet: offering his possessions, his actions and himself sacrificially (since no creature can produce a new thing for the Creator of all things); and giving glory to God, by song and action, for himself and for all others. Further, he was to have the God-like privilege of building, establishing and conducting, as a responsible co-worker under God, what we call civilization, and, finally, of sharing directly in the Life of God in the Beatific Vision: prosecuting the arts of making and of governing so skillfully and charitably as to make all earth a paradise and to win admission to the eternal Paradise.

That he might attain these ends, he was given the grace and the natural powers of cogitation which should have enabled him to deal with the problems of his city far more successfully than the bee, to choose but one example, deals with those of his hive: man's solutions were to be arrived at, not by the promptings of blind instinct, but by the guidance of grace-illumined reason; they were not to be guesses; they were to be sound hypotheses. For man had, originally, an "integrity" infinitely surpassing that of the highest animals.

But through a proud desire for too much knowledge, man lost the grace and thereafter the integrity—particularly, the cooperation of his powers in the performing of acts of skill—required for his due fulfilling of his functions as priest, prophet, maker and ruler.

From this condition of darkness, despair, perversity and ineptitude, man was rescued by God when in another act of astounding generosity (for God had no need of man's service and no obligation to rescue him in this way) He sent His Divine Son, Whose self-immolation won for man a loftier privilege than he had ever enjoyed before, the privilege of participating in Sonship. In and through Christ, man could once again fulfill the functions of priest, prophet, maker and ruler, this time in an infinitely higher way than ever.

The Catholic is therefore called upon to master, in accordance with his particular talents and opportunities, the various arts required for these functions: he is called upon to master the arts required for building up the Mystical Body of Christ and for sharing, as a member either of the ordained or of the lay priesthood, in the priesthood of Christ, whereby all the members of Christ's Body, the Church, are enabled to offer acceptably all that they are and all that they do, even their failures, to God the Father in the Spirit of Love. The Catholic must strive to master the arts of meditation and contemplation, along with the pure sciences that pertain to them, the better to voice a grateful praise of God for himself and for all other creatures. Further, as "another Christ," he must strive to attain eloquence in order that he may effectively spread the Good News (the *Evangelium*).

He is called upon to master, as well as he may, all the skills (and, naturally, the pure sciences that govern the development and use of these skills) that are required by the economic, the political, and the social orders. He is to be trained, therefore, to be a scientific artist in all the arts required for establishing and sacramentalizing civilization and for transforming whatever occupation he is destined to follow into a vocation, making himself scientifically proficient in the arts of living, that he may prosecute these for the love of God and neighbor, as well as his talents and circumstances permit.

That he may become truly skillful (a true artist at whatever he undertakes) he must give himself the leisure to master *liberally*, as if they were complete ends in themselves, all the fundamental sciences required by these arts of full Christian living. His attitude toward these studies must not be that either of the mental glutton or of the mere utilitarian; for neither of these attitudes is, in the end, spiritually sound or sufficiently practical. The Christian is a liberal artist—that is, a truly scientific and philosophic one—if for no other reason than that he must be so if he wishes to "use" his knowledge for discovery, for invention, or for contemplation as skillfully and as charitably as he should use it.

It is this view of the cosmos, of man's function in it, and of man's nature which determines the pattern of Catholic education; it is this view which dictates the method of training, the curriculum, and the teaching staff. Thus, the fact that the student is to be made into an artist suggests that he is to be given the kind of training best suited to the producing of artists—the apprenticeship (which, in its palest form is what is now called the case-method). Again, the fact that through original sin the student's powers have been not so much corrupted as disrupted means that he can best be trained mentally in the same way in which he is best trained athletically: he can best be induced to correlate his powers, not by taking calisthenic exercises for the strengthening of each of them individually, but by the execution of whole normal tasks which perfect them all cooperatively: the unity of the skill, like psycho-physical correlation, coming from the unity of the whole actions in which that skill is exercised.

The Catholic college of liberal arts, then, should be a community of workshops in which are learned the arts of conducting and sacramentalizing civilization; workshops in which artists-in-residence develop in their apprentices one or other scientifically grounded skill—this, by guiding them in their attempts to solve a unified and progressively more difficult array of normal problems. The training here is not simply in investigating what others have said or in learning how things are done; it is also a training in meditating on the truths of wisdom and in learning how to do things.

The curriculum must obviously include all the religious arts, as well as the major secular arts, each art being carefully integrated with every other. Philosophy and theology are central for the reason that if great skill can be most surely developed only under the guidance of the scientific principles that underlie rules-of-thumb, so too, the greatest skill can be developed only under the guidance of the philosophic and theological principles which underlie the scientific.

And the teacher in a Catholic college must, like every other true master, be trained to be what he is showing his apprentice how to become: a heroic, scientific, philosophic, and religious artist, living a profoundly contemplative and richly productive Christ-life in striving, under Christ, to establish and inspire others to establish the Kingdom spoken of in the preface to the Feast of Christ the King, the *regnum veritatis et vitae; regnum sanctitatis et gratiae; regnum justitiae, amoris et pacis.*

IV

The End: Vocational Living

WITH a general sketch of Catholic education before us, we can now proceed to a detailed consideration, one by one, of each of its major determinants. And since the first and most important determinant of any scheme is its purpose, we turn here to a study of the purpose of Catholic education, which is to train students for a way of life that is vocational.

This fact becomes clear, I believe, when we raise and answer the question: What do we mean, in the fullest or broadest sense, by a vocation; and what kind of training does it imply?

We are not, of course, concerned here primarily with what is perhaps most frequently meant by a vocation, or with the training that prepares for it; we are not primarily concerned with a call to the priesthood or to the religious state. Decisions raised by vocations like these are likely to be so delicate and so special as to be most fittingly dealt with by spiritual advisers and ecclesiastical authorities, rather than by deans and teachers as such.

Even here, however, the school or the college authorities must, to be sure, play their part, which, though indirect, is still large. Deans and teachers should feel obligated in this matter to this extent at least, that they must do nothing to prevent their charges from making a sound decision in considering the choice of a religious vocation, and they must do everything to aid them in making this decision. The least that educational authorities can do is prevent a student from getting either an inadequate or a "rosy" view of the priest-hood or the religious life: a view of it as pietistic, or escapist, or puritanical, or impractical, or unnatural, or disciplinarian. Courses in religion or philosophy, extra-classroom activities, customs, anything which may give students the impression that religion is mainly a matter of truculent apologetics and perfervid devotions may well cause them to believe that unless they have some skill in apologetics, some desire to be spiritual drill sergeants, or some talent in performing meditative ex-ercises of purely personal devotion, they could not have a vocation. The result is that the priesthood and the religious orders undoubtedly fail very often to gain the consideration of many of their finest potential recruits—simply because these have not always been given a sufficiently profound, un-sentimental, apostolic and heroic view of their religion, and an intensely joyful appreciation of its supernal beauty.

The truth is that the more clearly every student comes to see the full depth and dignity of the life of the ordinary Christian, the more clearly does he also come to see the spe-cial depth and dignity of the life of the extraordinary Chris-tian. No state of the Christian life can be adequately de-fined by a simple isolation of it; each state is best appreciated when defined comparatively, correlatively, and complemen-tarily with the others.

All educational authorities, then, may be said to have a common obligation to assure at least that tenor and atmos-phere of academic life which makes the choice between the religious and lay states of life as sound and as easy as possible. But the guidance of students into this or that lay vocation raises a set of problems calling for special studies, and it is with these that we are mainly concerned here.

Now, to see clearly what a vocation, in its broadest sense, is, we must, I think, go back to ultimate presuppositions—

to the facts and truths on the basis of which we may feel sure that any and every man can be thought of as having a vocation. The presuppositions are, it seems to me, the following:

1. God created a cosmos which is "organic"; one in which every creature has its own part to play in maintaining itself, in preserving its own order of being, its own kind, and by interdependence, every other order and kind of being. All creatures are "called" to perform these functions, and to perform them in such a way that they thereby declare the glory of God.

2. God, in creating man, created a special order of being (a fourth, above the mineral, vegetable and brute orders).[1] Unlike the other creatures, man was called to fill out the pattern of the cosmos, not merely by multiplication and adjustment, but by conscious and voluntary cooperation with the Creator; working with God, he was to complete and perfect one part of that cosmos, the part we call civilization. Man was not to establish and complete the human world in the same way in which the ants and the bees, for instance, establish and complete the insect world; he was to have a special favor, that of using all creatures, himself included, in accordance with their own natures, and with the law of the cosmos so as to develop and perfect an earthly kingdom of which he was to be the vice-regent under God, his King.

3. In carrying out his task, man was to be heedful that he use all things efficiently, justly, and religiously. He was to be an authority—an auctor—one who increases the power or effectiveness of that which he uses or governs. He was therefore to educe from the other creatures those energies needed for the construction of his own kingdom. But he was to do so justly, never forcing, coercing or rendering extinct any order of being; it is not his right to upset the pattern of the cosmos.

[1] As He also created a fifth above the human, the angelic.

Above all, he was to enable all creatures, his own kind particularly, to fulfill their loftiest function, the function of declaring the glory of God. In short, he was called from the first to be the one who should, in a sense, complete the pattern of the world, making all its orders into the citizenry or the co-citizenry of the Kingdom of God on earth. He was to be, under God, its maker, ruler, prophet, and priest.

4. That man was "called" to do these things we can feel sure, on the basis of both reason and revelation. Adam, made in the image and likeness of God, was given Godlike privileges and responsibilities; he was to make things, to rule creatures, and to maintain a kind of commerce, a commerce of love, with God Himself. Adam was called upon to dress the Paradise of pleasure, to exercise dominion over all the animals, to rule a household. He was to fill his needs by using creatures as his servants, and he was to exercise providential care in so doing. That he was to establish civilization and master the arts (the liberal arts) which it requires is obvious from several facts: first, man is social; second, each man has only certain talents, whether they be one, three or five; third, he is required to make the fullest use of these talents in serving other men, while living with them; and, fourth, the fullest use by men of their various kinds and numbers of talents implies the division of labor and the hierarchical governing of social bodies, both of which determine civilization.

Further, in the order of Redemption, every man is also called upon to be, in Christ, a priest and a prophet. He is a member of a royal priesthood, destined to restore all things in Christ, even at the cost of martyrdom. In accordance with his spiritual gifts (as St. Paul has pointed out) each man is called upon to increase and perfect the Mystical Body; he must help leaven the lump of civilization, doing so, as a member of the common priesthood, through his prayer, sacrifice and active participation in the Mass, performance of the corporal and spiritual works of mercy, as well as by his sacramentalizing of all his domestic, economic, political, and social activities.

5. We may say, in fact, that the very least "vocation" to which any layman is called includes the following:

—to be a saint through living the Christ-life;

—to help to build and perfect the Mystical Body;

—to share in the common priesthood;

—to share in the prophethood of Christ;

      as an apostle,

      as a witness and possible martyr;

—to carry out Catholic Action when called on by the hierarchy to do so.

—to use his powers to the full in making things and institutions, in managing them, and in sacramentalizing them, as well as in performing works of mercy.

—to do these things by following the "ordinary" rules of Christian charity, laid down for this "ordinary" way of life.

And the calling of the married layman is given a special dignity by the sacrament of matrimony and made to differ from this of the unmarried in three ways: he is to help increase the numbers of the Mystical Body by propagation; he is to establish and rule one institution in particular, the family, as a special unit of the Mystical Body (an *ecclesiola*); and he is to do so by following the rules of charity of the matrimonial way of life.

These, then, being the vocational objectives of the students with whom we are principally concerned, the next questions that arise naturally are, of course, the following: What must be the spirit in which these objectives are to be sought —the motivation? What methods of works are dictated by these objectives and this motivation? And what training can we give that will assure in our students the knowledge of these objectives, the proper spirit, and the required technical proficiency?

Obviously, the motive here must be that two-fold, intertwined love of God and neighbor, the proper name of which is Charity. Since this Charity is poured forth in our hearts by the Holy Spirit, Who is the Spirit of love in which the Father gives Love infinitely to the Son and the Son gives Love infinitely to the Father, so every vocation implies a spirit of self-donation. Whoever follows a vocation differs from others who carry on a business or a profession by the fact that he gives himself unstintingly, in Charity, to all whom he serves. To all whom he loves—and he loves everyone—he gives himself selflessly: to his wife, his children, his relatives, his friends, his fellow workers, his fellow citizens, his fellow members and potential members of the Mystical Body. To all he gives himself completely, yet in the order and the manner prescribed by God's laws. Thus he serves mankind in a spirit of self-donation truly marital, that he may offer himself and this service, in a similar spirit, to God.

Clearly, the motives of the commercialist, or even of the humanist, are not adequate for a true vocation carried on in this spirit of charity. How can they be? The commercialist, giving only with reluctance, or in hope of return (accounting his charity as good advertising)—such a man is not giving at all. He is, at worst, yielding to pressure, or, at best, "making an investment in good-will." Certainly, offering up part of one's success to God, like interest on a loan, or like the premium on a policy for insuring continued success, is hardly acting in the spirit of a vocation. God is not interested in being thrown a sop, or in being given a "cut" on a selfishly acquired fortune, however "generous" that cut may be. And the humanist, who gives, not himself with unreserved love, but his services and goods in accordance with distributive justice, with the measure of the Golden Mean and with the dictates of honor: he, too, may be little moved by that Spirit of boundless generosity by which every Christian must pray to be moved in all his actions.

To the Catholic, indeed, no merely calculating view of his occupation or way of life is possible; his philosophy and theology work together to convince him of that fact. For, all things are called—(if only in the sense of being called forth from nothingness into being and into playing a role in an ordered universe)—all things are called to be as God-like as possible. As St. Thomas has said: "The individual nature of a thing consists in the way in which it participates in the perfections of God." Since we are therefore most ourselves when we are most in the image and likeness of God, Who is love, we are most ourselves when we are most loving. In asking us to love one another, St. John is, in fact, not simply giving patriarchal advice; he is also asking us to live in accord with our fundamental nature as man and with our privileged status as Christians.

Now, such motivation inevitably results in the transforming of all occupations into professions in the fullest sense of the word. Those men who, in Charity, set out to make things or perform services as well as possible, soon discover that if they are to produce things of value to sell for a fair price, they will do well to form an association of masters in each of the crafts. They must lay down laws governing the quality of materials and workmanship. They must practice their craft with the utmost use of talent and skill. They must assure the perfecting of it as a scientific art. Since the apprenticeship system is ideal for training, they must establish workshops which are also schools for training future masters equally skilled and just.

They must be as charitable to their apprentices as to one another, practicing the corporal and spiritual works of mercy in their regard. They must profess a code of charity and justice superior to that of Aesculapius. Further, a little investigation will show that any activity, from garbage-collecting on up, is at least a craft and can be made into something of an art. (Require the doctors, lawyers, professors and clergy to collect the garbage on some one day every month—and it will be evident in no great time just how much of an art this occupation can become. And were similar tasks of "common labor" assigned to these groups, we could expect a similar proof of the fact that all forms of work can be made into arts.) Since slovenly work is nothing that we should presume to ask God the Son to offer us in the Spirit of love to God the Father; since, indeed, we are expected to make full use of our talents; and since the full and charitable use of these talents can only be assured by a Christianly professional system of making and exchange: it must be clear that the transforming of every occupation, whether basket-weaving, banking, or street cleaning, into a vocation, implies developing it as fully as possible into a scientific art and a profession. It implies, in fact, a technological apostolate.

The characteristics of a vocation, then, are these:

First, it is a calling. Every Christian is called upon and privileged to be a *coadjutor Dei*. Second, this calling consists primarily in establishing and conducting civilization in such a way as to transform it into the Kingdom of God on earth. Third, this task implies the spread and perfecting of the leaven —the Mystical Body; hence it implies a primary dedication of every Christian to sacramental work and the sacramental apostolate: to the fulfilling, that is, of the functions of the common or of the ordained priesthood, as well as those of prophethood and of Catholic Action. Fourth, a vocation implies the performing of all tasks in a spirit of self-donation, analogous to that Holy Spirit in which the Father gives Himself to the Son and the Son gives Himself to the Father. Fifth, this spirit prompts one to give only of one's best; consequently, it implies the transforming of all occupations into scientific arts and all trade unions into associations whose members profess a code of justice and Charity to all—that is, into professions in the fullest sense of the word. A vocation is, in short, a sacramental, dedicated, charitable, and skillful way of life to which, on the basis of the talents, disposition, and opportunities He has provided, one is called by God.

All this being so, we face now the question: what would be the ideal training for a vocational way of life? What, in particular, would be the kind of guidance it necessitates? What steps must we take to assure this ideal education and this ideal guidance—or, at least, to approximate them?

Obviously, the ideal education here would be one which made a student as skillful as possible in the arts he requires for being the priest-prophet-maker-ruler that he is supposed to be, no matter what his occupation. He should be made as skillful as his talents permit in all the arts of worship, in the executing of corporal and spiritual works of mercy, in propagating through the fine arts the truths of Wisdom, in craftsmanship, scientific discovery, and invention, in the conduct of business or politics. He should be, as a Christian, professional; and, as a professional, Christian.

All of which means, concretely, that he will be able to take part intelligently in dialogue and sung Masses, knowing the Latin and the Gregorian chant required for these highest forms of prayer. He will know his religion as something to be appreciated and lived, not merely as something to be defended or explained. He will have acquired skill in meditating, in praying with the Universal Church, in disposing himself aptly for the sacraments, and for producing and enjoying their fruits. He will be enthusiastic for and adept at the various forms of Catholic Action. As having had the basic (the "boot-camp") training of a soldier of Christ, he will be prepared for advancement in either way of life, religious or secular. Nor will he be a mere specialist in any one art or set of arts; he will be given general training in the fundamentals of all the arts and special training (by the case-method) in the vital technique peculiar to each art. In much the same way as pre-medical training is designed to prepare the student for the vocation of medicine (whether he is to become a pediatrician, a surgeon, or a general practitioner) so liberal arts training should prepare him for living as a Christian whatever his future occupation, whether it be the supervising of a foreign mission, the managing of a baseball team, or the directing of a forestry department.

And what is said here concerning the education of the young man applies with equal force to the education of the young woman. She, too, should be trained to do all things professionally—to make a profession of being a wife and mother, as well as of being a nurse or a nun. She is to become charitably professional in all her actions; and this, both positively and negatively.

Positively, she is to be made to see how difficult and noble, hence how supremely professional, the life of a homemaker can and must be. She is to be made to realize that if it requires great skill to be an exceptionally good teacher or nurse or diplomatist or interior decorator or dress-designer or storyteller or hostess or singer or purchasing agent or efficiency engineer or pediatrician or dietitian or chef or judge or mechanic, it certainly also requires even greater skill to be something of all of these by turns, as occasion demands. And to be all these in such a way as to make a home that will foster the saintliness of all who live in it—so that, for example, all its members re-joice on the day on which the favorite boy of the family an-nounces that he is going to become a Trappist, or the favorite girl that she is going to become a Carmelite—this requires a skill so great that "professional" seems too pale a word to do it justice.

Ideally, the Catholic young woman should be so trained, then, that having seen clearly what her profession consists in, she will subscribe intelligently, enthusiastically, and charitably to the code that it implies. She will hold herself strictly to the standard of high performance which it sets up. She will continue to develop her various kinds of skill by scientific and philosophic study, by experimentation and by attendance at conventions, local and national, on the problems of home-making. She will train not only her daughters, but any servants she may have—and train them scientifically and thoroughly, as apprentices. To these servants she will pay fair wages; and she will live in hope, not in fear, of the day when they become master home-makers in their own homes. And whenever it is necessary and possible for her to do so, she will charitably help in, or even take over, the households of the neighboring sick or needy.

Negatively, she should be trained to try and overcome everything that works counter to Christian professionalism: every form of commercialism and favoritism, whether it be that of relatives and friends, or of her husband or herself. She must, in other words, do everything she can to make sure that *all* members of society, not alone this or that section of it, may have the opportunity to live professionally and charitably.

This requirement will impose on her the duty of perform-ing certain not always pleasant acts of vigilance and self-denial. It will mean, for example, that she must learn to treat teachers, business men, politicians, as she now treats doctors—that is, as professional. Thus, she must try to assure that they be men, not merely of knowledge, but of skill—men who have served a strict apprenticeship and have demonstrated that they have the skill and the Charity necessary for their work. It will mean such things as that she will be suspicious of bargains, which are frequently the lure of the commercialist scheming to put the sound professional out of business; that she will not try to get her children into positions for which they have not been adequately (professionally) trained; or that she will not rest content at the sight of her son running a business unprofessionally—for profit alone. It will mean, finally, that in her voting and in her public life—in those duties to which the Pope has recently called her attention—she will ignore self-interest and act in a spirit of Christian patriotism, having a proper regard for the art of governing as a profession, and hence examining every candidate for office carefully, with these questions in mind: Does he regard his work as a profession? Does he try to enable others to live professionally and charitably? Or does he truckle to the powerful or pander to the mob?

But if, for one reason or another, a young woman is not destined to become a housewife or a nun, then she should try to enter one of the fields in which she can be expected as a woman to attain most naturally a certain professional excellence; since it is in this way that she can be sure of making the fullest and most charitable use of her powers. She should enter one of those occupations which are simply extensions, as it were, of one of the departments of home-making. Thus, she might become a doctor—especially a pediatrician—a dress-designer, a social worker, a manager of a rest home for the aged, a teacher, and so on. In occupations like these she could naturally attain a professional excellence and still be all woman, not an imitation man.

In short, our institutions should provide the young woman, as they should provide the young man, with basic training in the arts necessary for living abundantly and charitably at all times, whether in church or out. Her courses in Religion should make her, as his courses should make him, expert, not only in defending her Faith and in saying the Rosary or the Stations of the Cross, but also in participating deeply in the life of the Church, that is, in the life of Christ as it is lived by His Mystical Body throughout the Liturgical Year. By graduation time, it should be second nature for her, as it should be for him, to sing the chants which are the voice of the Church, to say the prayers of the Mass with the priest, to know what each Mass in succession means, to contemplate, with the guidance of the Breviary, each new phase of Christ's life during the year, to receive the sacraments and make full use of the sacramentals with a deep understanding of their significance; in brief, to be as alertly part of the Church as she is of her social circle—or, rather, much more so. Again, like his, her other courses should enable her to become professionally expert in the charitable management of secular affairs. None of these courses would be there mainly for her enjoyment or her future "success" or her advancement in the world; they would all be there to make her skillful at knowing, loving, and serving God, as well as her neighbor out of love for Him.

Here, as elsewhere, to be most effectively Catholic means to be most professionally Catholic, or, rather, to be most vocationally Catholic.

To this end, the one main thing, perhaps, for which those of us who are administrators or teachers should strive at present is the regaining and retaining of a proper technical concept of our work: we must try never to think of it as the dispensing of knowledge and the enforcing of regulations; we must see it as the training of apprentices and the building up of their morale. We must come to realize once more that we are, first of all, *masters of arts*—and secondarily expounders of sciences; that our students are our apprentices; that a liberal arts college is simply a well-integrated organization of selected workshops in the arts required for sacramental and professionally skillful living; that these workshops differ from ordinary craft workshops only because they train in the most essential acts required by the various arts mastered and because the training can be systematic, pedagogically ordered, scientific, and philosophic—rather than haphazard and rule-of-thumb. Moreover, we must give up the notion that we are primarily concerned with training the faculties of the student by making him exercise them on liberal *because* useless subjects and by making him "learn" principles—in the vague hope that he will then be able to find himself and his place in a chaotic world, through applying the principles he has memorized with a kind of instinctive rightness or tact. We must learn to give to mental calisthenics about the same esteem as that given by the physical trainers to physical calisthenics. For, just as no physical trainer would consider a man an all-round athlete who had merely practiced the essential movements of all athletics and memorized books of hygiene, but had seldom played football, baseball, basketball, etc., so must we not consider a man a liberal artist who has merely practiced the mental movements of all the arts and memorized the scientific principles underlying them, but has seldom tried to act as an ethician, an economist, a politician, a philosopher, a priest of the common priesthood. No form of exercise or training should, of course, be condemned outright; but we may well ask ourselves, I think, whether our colleges should not provide a training that would resemble much more closely than it does that of the obstacle course and of practice ma-

receives its name; with which Thou didst anoint Priests, Kings, Prophets, and Martyrs.

That for those to be made new by the Baptism of a spiritual cleansing, Thou mayest confirm this creature of Chrism as a sacrament of perfect health and life; that when the sanctifying ointment has been poured on them, and the corruption of their first birth swallowed up, then may the holy temple which each man has thus become be fragrant with the pleasant odor of innocence of life; that according to the Sacrament which Thou hast established, penetrated through and through with this kingly, priestly, and prophetic honor, they may be clothed with the vestment of an incorruptible gift of honorable office; that it may be to those who shall have been reborn of water and the Holy Spirit, a Chrism of salvation; and that it may cause them to be made partakers of eternal life and sharers of the glory of Heaven, through the same Jesus Christ, Thy Son, Who lives and rules with Thee in the unity of the same Holy Spirit, forever and ever. AMEN.

V

The End—By Contrast

THERE is perhaps no better way for us to bring home to ourselves the differences between the aims of Catholic education and other forms of education than by pausing for a moment, at this point, to consider these various aims one after another. In this chapter, therefore, we shall glance briefly at the aims of the naturalistic, the purely humanistic, and the Catholic forms of education.

Naturalistic, or, if you will, Rousseauistic educators, looking upon man as hardly more than a higher animal, limit their aims, logically enough, to training him for the satisfying of his passionate needs—his physical and mental desires. The law of progress seems to such educators, as it seems to most industrialists, to imply the multiplication of wants and the satisfaction of these through a "high" standard of living. Education, for them, consists largely in the training of students for a sensitive appreciation of more and more luxuries, as well as for a mastery of the information required for the producing of these luxuries. They consider that student well educated who has a due gusto, a due sensitiveness, a due discrimination for the enjoyment of life as a connoisseur; who has good sense enough not to worry about, and humility enough to treat as inscrutable, the ultimate problems of philosophy and religion; taste enough to delight in the wise melancholy of Omar Khayyam or Montaigne, the glamor of Shakespeare, and the "macabre idealism" of Dante; technical skill enough to invent something that is in universal demand; and religious feeling

48

enough to conduct humanitarian drives. The romantic, positivistic, and pragmatic methods which produce this kind of
person must therefore be ideal.

The other group of educators, the humanistic, seem far
less epicurean than the naturalistic; but, for that very reason,
their ideals may prove far more dangerous. Humanists, looking
upon man as primarily a moral, rather than a spiritual, creature, limit their educational aims, with apparent reasonable-
ness, to the attainment of what might be called wise character.
Happiness, if we are to believe the humanists, results from the
establishment and conduct of a temperate civilization, all the
members of which would be, according to their capacities,
men of traditional culture, of decorous custom, and of humble
self-control. Institutions run wisely and humanly by men of
natural prudence, temperance, justice, and fortitude; lives
that, as a consequence, are happy because in accord with the
laws of the cosmos and of human nature as part of the cosmos;
these, the humanists tell us, are the true aims of education,
any other aims being dangerously immoderate or illusory.
Thinking to avoid the sub-rationality and the cynical despair
of the romantic and pragmatic, on the one hand, and the wishful presumption of the religious, on the other, the humanists
propose as ideal that form of education which produces the
gentleman of broad and time-tested culture who lives by the
law of the golden mean. The wise man, it appears, is he who is
always on the alert against cherishing anything, no matter
what it may be, too hopefully, too seriously, too enthusiastically, or too lovingly—even when that thing is the well-at-
tested Charity of God Himself in sending His Son for the
redeeming and dignifying of humanity. The education, therefore, in which the teachers provide intellectual and moral
training in the arts of civilization according to the principles
to be found in the great works of the past to students who

discipline themselves in meditation and self-control: this is the education which the humanist proposes as the best possible.

Now, even if there were no other motives for doing so, this consideration, one after another, of these views of education should cause us to haul ourselves up short whenever we find that we are adopting them or following them unsuspectingly. Merely setting them against the Catholic view should of itself prove decisive. Even if it were not obvious to us that any attempt to educate which has its focal point in man rather than in God is in tendency sinful and so doomed to ultimate failure; whereas, in fact, in education, as in everything else, the seeking of the Kingdom of God and His justice means that all things will be added to us;—even if these great truths were not clear to us, we should still see how pale and inadequate the naturalistic and humanistic forms of education appear, even at best, against the truly divine splendor of the Catholic. For we possess, in the truths revealed to us by God Himself and clarified for us by His saints and His vicars, the most profound, because the most spiritual, view of education that is possible. Ours, indeed, should more properly be termed not a view at all, but a vision.

We may see our work as aimed at turning out young men and young women who will translate the life of Christ into the idiom of their own lives, doing what they can to form a society in which all men will pursue their work as a kind of vocation, in a spirit of sacrificial charity that will impel them not only to sacramentalize all things and bring them to a head in Christ, but to do this as well, as artistically, as possible. For, is not the society at which, as Catholics, we are aiming a society in which artists[1] in discovery will aid artists in

---

[1] In the sense, of course, of "liberal artists"—men whose skill is the result of scientific and philosophic discipline.

communication and invention to produce goods which artists in production and distribution, guided by artists in government, will pass on to all their fellow members—all working contemplatively, charitably, and sacramentally, in cooperation with the hierarchy, not only for the establishment of civilization, but for the growth and perfection of Christ's Mystical Body?

To dismiss this vision as too religious, or to dismiss it as impractical simply will not do; since to accept it is only to accept the import of the great Encyclicals of the Popes from Leo XIII to the present. Consider the implications of these words of Pope Pius XI which stand at the beginning of his Encyclical on the Christian Education of Youth: "In fact, since education consists essentially in preparing man for what he must be and for what he must do here below, in order to attain the sublime end for which he was created, it is clear that there can be no true education which is not wholly directed to man's last end, and that in the present order of Providence, since God has revealed Himself to us in the Person of His Only-Begotten Son, Who alone is 'the way, the truth, and the life,' there can be no ideally perfect education which is not Christian education." Note also his answer to the charge that the education that is so directed is not practical. "The true Christian does not renounce the activities of this life; he does not stunt his natural faculties; but he develops and perfects them by coordinating them with the supernatural. He thus ennobles what is merely natural in life and secures for it new strength in the material and temporal order, no less than in the spiritual and eternal. This fact is proved by the whole history of Christianity and its institutions, which is nothing else but the history of civilization and progress up to the present day. It stands out conspicuously in the lives of the saints, whom the Church, and she alone, pro-

duces" (and let us note carefully the next phrase) "in whom
is perfectly realized the purpose of Christian education, and
who have in every way ennobled and benefited human society. Indeed, the saints have ever been, are, and ever will be
the greatest benefactors of human society, and perfect models
for every class and profession, for every state and condition
of life, from the simple and uncultured peasant to the master
of sciences and letters, from the humble artisan to the com-
mander of armies, from the father of a family to the ruler of
peoples and of nations, from simple maidens and matrons of
the domestic hearth to queens and empresses . . . Such are
the fruits of Christian education. Their price and value is derived from the supernatural virtue and life in Christ which
Christian education forms and develops in man."

VI

The Catholic Concept of the Main Obstacle

IF CHRISTIANITY shows us the general ends of education and presents us with the best models of its products, it also points directly to the main obstacle we have to deal with and the main need we have to keep in mind when we try to attain these ends and approximate these models.

That main obstacle, as Pope Pius XI has said, is Original Sin, just as the main need is the preparing of the student for the active, hence the most fruitful, reception of grace, and for active cooperation with that grace in all that he does in life.

To quote his exact words on these points, the Pope has said concerning Original Sin that "every method of education founded wholly or in part on the denial or the forgetfulness of original sin and of grace, and relying on the sole powers of human nature is unsound." And concerning the necessity of preparing the student for the reception of and cooperation with grace, he has said, to quote but one of many statements: "Disorderly inclinations, then, must be corrected, good tendencies encouraged and regulated from tender childhood, and above all the mind must be enlightened and the will strengthened by supernatural truth and the means of grace, without which it is impossible to control evil impulses, impossible to attain to the full and complete perfection of education intended by the Church, which Christ has endowed so rightly with divine doctrine and with the Sacraments, the efficacious means of grace."

If, with these key statements as a guide, we turn to explore the doctrine on the Garden of Eden, we shall begin to see the essential nature and main objectives of all truly Catholic education. For if we fix our eyes on the truths which St. Thomas teaches us concerning man's original state, concerning the Fall as disrupting his nature, and concerning the Mass and the Sacraments as restoring that nature, we shall then gain a clear view, not only of the source and magnitude of the difficulties we face in educating anyone, but also of the source and the magnitude of the forces to which we can have recourse.

Studying the Garden of Eden, we see immediately, at least if we look at it through the eyes of St. Thomas, that in this happy spot there would have been neither school nor teacher as we know them today. Every son of Adam, had his father not fallen, would, like every other creature on earth, have had all the powers necessary for living happily in accordance with his state. Since it was normal for man to live a supernaturalized life, he would have had all the powers he needed. Discovering each new truth as occasion demanded, he would have grasped the full import of it; that is, he would have done far more than simply know it; he would have realized it. Whatever he would have made, he would have made with grace-inspired ease and ingenuity; for he had the power of invention. And he would have possessed the integrity that would have enabled him to resist impulse and to check and coordinate all his faculties harmoniously and happily. He would have found it easy to learn for himself, to teach others, or to be taught everything that he needed to know when and as he needed to know it.

Let me dwell for a moment on these truths, so that we may see a little more clearly than we might otherwise just what they imply for us today.

I say that it was normal for man, not simply to know but

to *realize*; he knew, that is, as we ourselves know, when we say with an exclamation: "I realize that fully!" When he knew something, he knew it as existing, as the thing that it was, so well that, as the Bible says, he could name it—or to put this in modern terms—give a one-word definition of it. He saw its nature and what it signified of its cause, God. He saw the splendor of its design and of its rightness—its beauty, and this too as the refraction of God's. He saw what responsibility it implied for him; how good it was; what rights it had; what duties towards it he had to fulfill; how it was a reflection of God's Holy Goodness. In short, when he understood something, he gained far more than a scientific knowledge of it, or even a metaphysical; he was, as we say, struck by its full significance, so that he felt as well as grasped its being, its truth, its goodness, and its beauty and all that these implied, first in relation to God, and then in relation to all creaturehood.

I said also that he had the power of invention. And by this I meant that he could instinctively find the right solution to the problems of making tools, language, institutions, and the like, because his instincts (his cogitative sense, to be technical[1]) were not potentially, but actually under the guidance of the intellect. His hunches were intellectually sound. His reason was governed by a sound instinct, his instinct by a sound reason. What we call, in describing a good craftsman today, "a matter of second nature with him" was, with Adam before the Fall, literally a matter of first nature. In solving his problems, he needed no critic, because he obeyed subconsciously, ahead of time, the principles which he could easily have pointed out and justified afterwards.

His power of learning was as great as his power of making. Having an unspoiled mind, its faculties all duly working to-

[1] For a description of the cogitative sense and its work, see Chapters 9 and 10.

gether, he would have needed only to have each new situation about which he was to learn slightly arranged or staged, as in a good joke or parable, for him to see and enjoy seeing the point, and for him to put it into practice unerringly.

Morally, also, man in the state of nature would have been an ideal learner. He would have been well poised, rather than easily thrown off balance. Such a man would not have easily been hypnotized by the appearances of things into a blindness to their true nature, or into a lust for abusing them. Seeing them and feeling them as they are—understanding and responding to them duly—he would have dealt with them intelligently, justly, temperately, lovingly, rather than superficially, coldly, lustfully, or sentimentally.

And except for the wiles of the Tempter and his own pride, he should never have sought to eat with his mind more than he needed as he needed it. He would never have committed the sin which many today have forgotten is a sin, the sin of intellectual curiosity. He would never have allowed the desire for knowledge for its own sake to seduce him from communion with God at all times. An integrated person, he would have found his soul equipped with harmonious powers of knowing and inventing, and directed by a will inspired by grace, so that he would have been in contact and concord with God in all his actions.

Since it was normal for man in his original state to live supernaturally, but only on condition of his not turning away from the Source of supernatural life, when, at the Fall, man did so turn away, he lost the integrity and the spiritual energy which up until then had made him easy to educate. He was no longer the grace-inspired, scientific craftsman, having the lordship of true authority over all creatures. He became, rather, the one thing on earth that was positively chaotic, proudly specialistic, and scientific rather than wise; above all, ill poised, passionate, gluttonous, the prey of the great Seducer and all his fanatic slaves. With the loss of the grace for supernatural living, man turned away from that grace itself; and he became a confederation of individualistic faculties, each fighting for more than its due rights, and each, to that extent, harming the others.

Man, therefore, became unable to resist the blandishments of not only his lustful and intemperate fellow men, but of nature itself. He fell prey to the isolated desires of his various faculties. He began to be positively proud of being called an intellectual, or a man of strong will, or a sensitive soul, or a great reasoner, or a man of sound judgment, or a man of action. He even forgot his own spiritual nature in his sorry content with his own narrow excellence; and he began to lose hope that God either could or would restore him to a state of grace in which he could trust all his powers again to cooperate.

Not that he became so much corrupted as disrupted; his natural powers were not gravely harmed intrinsically; and even his sound tendencies remained, although diminished. For, as St. Thomas says (Sum. Theol. 1a-2ae; Quaest. 85, Art 1), "When we speak of the good of nature, we may be referring here to any one of three things: First, we may be referring to the principles of nature, of which the nature is constituted, and the properties caused by these, such as the powers of the soul and the like. Second, we may be referring to the fact that because man has from nature an inclination towards virtue, as we have shown earlier, this inclination towards virtue is itself a good in nature. Third, we may be speaking of the good of nature called the gift of original justice, which was concentrated for all human nature in the first man. Now, the first of these goods of nature (that is, the principles of which it is constituted), has been neither diminished

nor taken away. But the third good (the gift of original justice) has been taken away wholly by the sin of the first Parent.
But the middle gift, that is, the inclination itself towards virtue is diminished by sin." He also says earlier (Quaest. 83),
"Original sin has first of all to do with the will." He is likewise careful to point out that the other powers which it affects
are primarily the concupiscible; and that it lessens the power
of reason by the fact that each new act of unreason, such as
sin, makes easier the next, though the power of reason itself
is never taken away, since even to sin we must reason (Quaest.
85, Art 2). It would seem, therefore, that whatever the harm
suffered by the individual faculties, the greatest harm was
that of the destruction of their powers of cooperation.

In the light of all these truths, then, namely: (1) That
man in actual fact is a creature who needs grace even for the
normal functioning of his natural powers. (2) That endowed
with the grace of original justice, he was marvellously virtuous
and skillful in the use of his powers. (3) That primarily he
was an artist, and only secondarily a scientist. (4) That he was
able to coordinate his powers easily. (5) That even after the
Fall, he still had his intellectual powers more or less unharmed.
(6) That just as, before the Fall, his powers worked together
with wonderful harmony in the performance of the feats for
which they were designed, namely, contemplation, understanding, governing and making, so, even after the Fall, his
powers retain these same tendencies, however diminished;—
in the light of all these truths, it becomes evident that the task
of any educator is primarily two-fold: that of trying to restore
his pupil somehow to a state in which he is once more in contact with the Source of grace, God; and that of training the
powers which are thus to be re-animated so as to strengthen
their tendencies to cooperate. For the Catholic educator, these
requirements mean specifically training the student to take full

advantage of the grace won for him by Christ, the grace of being a member of Christ's Own Mystical Body and of sharing sacramentally in His very Life; and aiding him to regain an inner harmony of his faculties by giving him an apprenticeship in the kind of artistic feats which will assure the use of all his faculties hierarchically in the performance of normal duties. In a sense, therefore, all education is, for the Catholic, re-education, and all training is a form of occupational therapy with Christ the main Physician-Teacher.

VII

The Catholic Concept of the Student

IF, AS OUR study thus far would seem to show, Catholic educators should be guided by the following exigencies: that they
train the student for his particular vocation as priest-prophet-
maker-ruler; that they train him to fulfill this in truly professional and vocational spirit; that, in so doing, they treat
Original Sin as their main obstacle;—then it is fairly clear
under what various aspects they are to regard the student.
Thus, it is fairly clear that, as needing to be trained for religious living, the student may be regarded as a disciple; as
needing to be trained to do everything with professional skill,
he may be regarded as an apprentice; as needing to be trained
in the acquisition of the knowledge required for such skill, he
may be regarded as scientist or scholar; as needing to be made
heroic, he may be regarded as a cadet; and as needing to be
kept mentally sound, he may be regarded as, in a sense, a
patient.

Our next step in clarifying our concept of Catholic education might well be, then, to observe just what, in general,
is implied by this multiplex way of viewing the student:—
How does it determine our notions, in general at least, of
what we are to expect of him? What does it suggest about the
best ways of motivating him? What, also, about curricula,
schedules, teaching-methods, and teacher-training?

First of all, obviously the condition of discipleship for
sanctity means, so far as the student is concerned, that his
training should be primarily and intrinsically religious. He

should be shown that the central objective of his education
and of his whole life should be that of furthering the spread
and perfecting the activity of the Mystical Body of Christ,
devotedly sharing whatever grace he may receive with others,
and allowing the Christ-life to express Itself through the idiom
of his own. Self-centered interest in his own improvement or
advancement; the pleasures of the dilettante; the love of luxury and ease; proud exultation in self-expression; the delight
in honor: these are not for him. His motivation should become thoroughly supernatural: in him the infused virtues of
Faith, Hope, and Charity, of prudence, justice, temperance,
and fortitude, strengthened by the Gifts of the Holy Spirit,
are to take over, as it were, his natural virtues and enable him
to produce the Fruits of the Holy Spirit. Humbly losing himself in the Mystical Body, he is to regain himself there; his
skill, animated by Charity, being put to the service of Charity.

To these ends, his training, his curriculum, his very schedule, should be planned to make him expert, first of all, as a
Catholic; expert, both as one who knows his religion thoroughly and as one who lives it thoroughly. The sound Catholic student should be at least as learned in the truths of Faith
as in the truths of reason; at least as familiar with word of
God as with the word of man. Nor, if he is to be in the proper
sense studious, should he ever study to satisfy mere curiosity,
this form of gluttony being no more excusable, even when it
is intellectual, than is any other form. On the contrary, the
Catholic student, while learning to appreciate every being for
its own truth, goodness, and beauty, should also learn to value
it as enabling him to appreciate the truth, goodness, and beauty
of God and fellow-men and as equipping him to serve them
better. Moreover, he becomes a person exceptionally skilled
in worshipping God in the manner in which God wishes to

wishes to acquire, not merely knowledge, but skill; and this in any and all acts of worship, of conduct, and of making. He is animated by the desire of the true professional to meet the need of a patron perfectly; he takes delight in the exercise of his skill, but greater happiness in the rightness and beauty of the thing he produces. Not money, not honor, not pride in work; none of these is for him a primary motive; his chief aim is the making of things as well as possible, that he may thereby be as charitable as possible.

These aims mean that the student is trained in the fundamentals of the arts of making, of conducting affairs, of sacramentalizing, meditating, contemplating, and worshipping, so that he finds himself at home in them and well equipped with the habits which they require. He is given, ideally, not only an apprenticeship in each art, but also one in the general philosophy of all craftsmanship and art, thus learning to obey, as a matter of second nature, the principles common to every feat of invention and action, as well as those peculiar to any one kind of invention and action.

The ordering of his work, as well as his schedule, must, as a consequence, resemble much more that of a football team than that of a sight-seeing tour: the order in which an apprentice learns best is seldom "logical"; nor can the kinds and the amounts of the information he is to be given be fixed inflexibly; these things must be determined by the quickness with which he both "catches on" and matures. Roughly, about two-thirds of his time must be given over to practice, his curriculum and schedule both being determined more by the requirements of familiarization and performance than by those of memorizing and test-taking.

Viewed under his next most important aspect, that is, as being concerned with the acquiring of knowledge, the student is properly to be considered a young scientist. As that, he has for his main objective the acquisition of skill in discovering, distilling, and remembering truths—those truths especially which will enable him to be, not a rule-of-thumb, but a *scientific* artist in making, in sacramentalizing, in meditating, and in worshipping. His proper motive, purely as a scientist, is the love of truth and order, his delight being the beauty of creatures and, by implication, of God, as this beauty shines through the principles of nature seen in action: his is the delighted wonder at the radiant perfection of God's making as this is manifested throughout the whole cosmos, mankind and civilization included.

Here, then, the student is to be given the experience of working, as a scientist, in various sciences on various levels of knowledge: coming in this way to know, by first-hand experience, such things, for instance, as what it means to classify, define, hypothesize, experiment, formulate, verify, check, evaluate, correlate, and expound; what is meant by the difference between the science of necessary matter and that of contingent; what the differences are between the science which studies things as they are given; that which studies things as they ought to be; and that which studies the norms of things as they can be made to be (the natural, the normative, and the technical); what the differences are between the levels of physics, cosmology, ontology, and theology; what the differences are between the methods of induction, deduction, and inductive descent; and so on. And what is not least important, the student also gains the power to correlate, as well as differentiate, his various studies, uniting them as well as distinguishing them.

The fourth condition of the student, cadetship, is that wherein he is assured of the morale, as well as the skill, neces-

sary for performing the feats required of him as a hero helping
to "redeem the time." Under this aspect, he has for his objective that of chivalrously devoting himself to the charitable,
loyal, fearless, and enthusiastic service of God and fellowmen,
acting here in the capacity of what Father William Leonard,
S.J., has called the combat-engineer of the Church Militant.
He sees himself as building the City of God under fire, willingly risking martyrdom to establish "the peace of Christ in
the reign of Christ." He is motivated by a fortitude born of
Charity in all its forms: the love of the Trinity, of Christ
Crucified, of His Blessed Mother, of His Church, of the saints,
of all his fellow Christians, of fellow-men, all in the image and
likeness of God, and of all God's creatures. And his main inspiration as a soldier of Christ is the Apocalypse showing him
in what sense he is at war, against what forces, towards what
final conquest.

His training therefore is at least as ascetic as that of the
cadet in a military school, being designed to enable him to
perform more and more complex feats, with greater and
greater responsibility, to meet higher and higher standards,
under more and more trying conditions. He is not, of course,
to be treated as a mere Spartan: he is to be neither strained
by an attempt to do the well-nigh impossible, nor made to
take a merely grim or sardonic delight in overcoming obstacles. Rather he must be encouraged to rejoice in and re-
fresh himself at the springs of Beauty: being recreated by the
Beauty of God and of His creation, refreshed by the splendor
of the cause to which he is devoting himself, as well as of the
rightness of his achievements. His courses in the various fine
arts fill him with delight at the radiant beauty of God's power
and goodness and fire him with a happy enthusiasm for what
he knows is right. In his every course, indeed, he is made to
appreciate intensely the beauty of every sacramentalized ac-

tion as well as the technical beauty of everything that has been made or performed skillfully.

His schedule must therefore give the leisure required for spiritual joy: as far as possible, all his courses, especially his courses in philosophy and religion, are to be enjoyed, rather than endured—just as his arduous training for the football team is enjoyed rather than endured. Certainly, he is never to feel that these subjects are to be regarded as a form of calisthenics, pointless in themselves but useful as a means of mental drill. He is no more to feel that college is a place where one is under continuous pressure than he is to feel that it is a place for loafing. His must be the happy disposition of the good athlete "in training."

Finally, the Catholic student, as a redeemed son of Adam, learns to regard and treat himself as in some sense a convalescent, keeping before his mind the attaining of integrity, so as to become as sound a member of the Mystical Body as possible. His motivation here is the desire for inner peace and for that rightness befitting to a creature in the image and likeness of God, another Christ, and the main instrument which he, himself, has to use in the service of Charity. His curriculum and training must be so designed as to enable him to discover his abilities and deficiencies and to acquire the knowledge necessary for handling himself well in difficult emotional crises. He must, in other words, be given an un-self-conscious knowledge of himself and of what to do about himself. And his schedule must make provision for the experiences whereby he acquires this self-knowledge, as well as for periods of convalescence after emotional crises; he must have the leisure for determining, analyzing, and adjusting himself to his mental or emotional ills—for "coming to," for "making a fresh start," and for "bringing himself along" easily. He must always have a reasonable opportunity to catch up with his fellows, under special tutoring and guidance. For if it is only right that a student should be specially cared for who has suffered a concussion of the brain, it is likewise only right that a student should be specially cared for who has suffered a concussion of the mind or of the heart.

VIII

The Catholic Concept of the Teacher

CORRESPONDING to the Catholic student as disciple, apprentice, young scientist, cadet, and convalescent, the Catholic teacher may be viewed as a combination of spiritual master, master artist, master scientist, leader, and therapist.

First, as spiritual master—that is, as having under him a number of disciples—the Catholic teacher is obliged, no matter what his field, to do what he can to inspire in his students a love of the Church, to give them an appreciation of its spirit, as well as of its externals; so that their minds may become naturally one with the mind of the-Church: Her truth, their truth; Her sacrifice, their sacrifice; Her speech, their speech; Her songs, their songs; Her worship, their worship; Her life, their life. A master of student-disciples must do this lovingly, adapting with care his means to their state of spiritual development, as did Our Lord with His disciples. The main "lessons," if they can be called that, being personal talks, the spirit of Wisdom and Charity is thus imparted by a system which might be called that of Socrates were it not better called, through our Lord's sanction of it, God's own tutorial system. The association of disciples with masters in grace-filled and joyful *symposia*: here is the ideal. The privilege of doing some of this teaching may, perhaps, be granted to upper classmen for their proficiency; but whoever the masters may be, they must always strive, in dealing with their students as disciples, to be as simple in their methods, as natural, as humanly poetic, as considerate, and as loving as was Our Lord.

These requirements naturally imply that in knowledge,

68

skill, and spiritual maturity, the masters must be at least as adept as the disciples are to become by graduation time. They must themselves have lived the liturgy, skillfully as well as whole-heartedly. They must have experienced *growth* into becoming a sound Member of the Mystical Body; they must have reached a state in which they discover to their surprise that it is a matter of habit with them to meditate, contemplate, sacramentalize, and so on. Being thus deeply experienced in the arts of Christian living they can then, in dealing with young and inexperienced followers, prove, in the literal sense of the word, *expert*. Above all, they must be so charitable that every student will think of them as being animated by kindness itself, which is the Holy Spirit.

Nor will any sound teacher, imbued with the love of God and of his students, hold back from teaching at all times on as high a level as possible: the fear that he may talk above his students' heads will be balanced by the realization of the fact that to sin, as St. Bonaventure and St. Augustine say, is not to cherish the bad, but to prefer the lesser good. The true teacher feels that to the extent to which he gets his student-disciples to reach, not merely some, but the highest levels, to just that extent will he have succeeded. And his charity and love of all things that are good will be in him so unaffected and habitual, so easy and natural, that his disciples will come to take for granted the reality, the rightness, and the *attainableness* of spiritual excellence. He will, in fact, be thorough master of one of the greatest arts of teaching: that of assuming his students into their better selves.

As having charge of apprentices, the Catholic teacher looks upon himself as a master of an art of which he is to make his student also a self-reliant master. His tasks are therefore those of reproducing ideally the conditions under which an in-expert beginner can acquire a versatile skill gradually, surely, hopefully, self-reliantly, enthusiastically. As far as possible, then, the teacher must introduce the young beginner to the problems and methods of the given liberal art in the same way in which the 14th or 15th Century Flemish master of painting introduced his apprentices to this particular fine art —the main differences between the two being, ideally, those of degree rather than kind: the problems and methods of the workshop having the force of reality, since they were those of an actual assignment or job; and the problems and methods in the college course having the efficiency of systematic and pedagogical arrangement. Thus, the teacher must try to put the student through the experience of becoming a master, not merely of seeing or learning what the master knows, assigning real feats of investigation, invention, communication, meditation, communal worship, to be accomplished somehow at first and better and better as the student familiarizes himself with them and grows into the ability to perform them. Although the problems of each art will be set and orderly, as determined by the major feats of that art (just as the problems of football are determined by the playing of a series of games for a season), they will always be regarded first of all as problems: the apprentice will always be required to try and solve them on his own—"as originals," to use the phrase of the geometry teacher—recognizing and adopting a solution only after having tried to arrive at one, never merely memorizing a solution except for the convenience of its exact formulation. Nor will the apprentice be given any more mental calisthenics than is the football player given physical calisthenics: skill is mainly perfected by being exercised on complete, proper, whole tasks such as are really called for, however small these tasks may be. Above all, the teacher, being an enthusiastic and creative master of his art, will, again like a good football coach, inspire in his students a relish for shop-talk; and what is the deepest and most delightful shop-talk of a liberal art but the science, the philosophy, and the theology of it?

Each department head, in the ideal Catholic college, must see to it that at least the honor students—preferably, of course, all the students—have the privilege of working under a practising expert—some artist-in-residence, if you will—who is being subsidized by the college in his carrying out of a real and vital project. Students, to say nothing of their instructors, must be given the privilege, in other words, of working under, collaborating with great experts in the performing of real feats, whether these be of scientific investigation, scholarly exegesis, philosophic investigation, invention, designing, writing, composing, social work, Catholic Action, or what not.

Naturally, this highly desirable condition means that every Catholic teacher, whether he is a so-called Master of Arts or not, must surely be a master of some one art, and that whether or not he is what is commonly called a Doctor of Philosophy he must certainly be a teacher of the love of wisdom (Doctor Philosophiae) as Wisdom is born of the profound mastery of an art. That such a teacher will be, in one sense at least, a great scholar, goes without saying: if a great stamp-collector is a great scholar of stamps, an equally great stamp designer is almost always an even greater scholar of them, to say nothing of his being a far greater teacher of how to appreciate them for their essential rather than their accidental qualities.

As being in charge of students, the Catholic teacher must, of course, train each one in what might be called studentship pure and simple, awakening him to the importance and delightfulness of a subject, showing him how to familiarize himself with it quickly and find his way about in it, how to compile information about it, take notes, appraise critically, make full use of language equipment, take advantage of libraries and other facilities—in brief, show him how to become a master scholar in the subject. Not only must the Catholic teacher have a thorough grasp of the subject which he teaches, he must also manifest a natural and intense appreciativeness of it, as well as of all sound learning; responding deeply to the fascination of it, he must, as it were, infect his students with a similar enthusiasm for it. Through his knowledge of pedagogy, his understanding of the methods of the feature article writer, the salesman, the dramatist, and the poet and through his tactful common-sense in applying these methods, he must be able to fire his students with that same kind of delighted interest in a liberal art which they have in their favorite sports; yet, in all this, never losing sight of the difference between curiosity and studiousness.

He must present every item of knowledge with great heed to the relation which it bears to all other knowledge which the student is acquiring, and to the student's purpose of leading a saintly and wise life. He must make clear to the student that every fact is always to be appreciated for its own sake, but is never to be appreciated for its own sake alone. (Indeed, it can be maintained that no one can fully appreciate a thing for itself until he has also seen it in relation to God.) The good teacher realizes, in other words, that every student should come forth from a liberal arts college with an ardent though not a "passionate" love for truth of all kinds—he should be scholarly, but without any desire whatsoever to function as an unusually convenient form of encyclopedia.

As an officer in charge of the cadets of the Church Militant, the Catholic teacher must know how to follow the methods of military discipline and military leadership analogically, so as to turn out true heroes in the ever-present battles between the forces of Christ and those of the Prince of this world. By every means at his disposal, the teacher-as-leader

must train his student to be able to resist the onslaughts of
the enemy; that is, never to lose his head and become an ap-
peaser or engage in battle only to flee in panic, hypnotized
by false fears, misled by false propaganda, weakened by worry
and ostracism, bewildered by spiritual fifth columnists, filled
with despair at his inability to achieve what the world calls
success. The teacher must know how to forestall such demoralization; he must, indeed, be an expert morale-builder,
all his disciplinary measures being calculated to fortify. He
must therefore see how all the greatest fine art, no matter of
what kind, has for its ultimate—though not, of course, for its
immediate—purpose this same effect of fortifying, through
edification and recreation of the soul. He must understand
how the enjoyment which a fine art affords, and affords so
cleverly as to appear to exist for no other reason, has always
for its highest and proper purpose that of disposing its appre-
ciators to cooperate with the Gifts of the Holy Spirit, so as to
produce the Fruits of the Holy Spirit and the graces of the
Beatitudes. He must, in short, master all the arts required for
making the student enjoy being a patriot of the Kingdom of
God; so that when any one of his students catches sight of the
Cross on a distant steeple, he will receive at least as great
a thrill of piety as does the West Pointer when he catches
sight of the flag waving on a distant flag-pole.

All of which comes down to saying that the same kind of
thing that has long been done at West Point and Annapolis,
as well as on our battlefields all over the world, can and must
be done in our colleges—and, indeed, much better; for our
discipline can call on Christian fortitude, rather than on
mere stoic self-reliance. Our students also can be notable
for their neatness, punctuality, orderliness, obedience, responsibility, steadiness, and esprit-de-corps, and, beyond all
this, for their self-denial, self-oblation, heroic Charity. They

can be, with God's grace, strong and ready for martyrdom, in the interests not only of the nation, but of Christendom.

Finally, as a therapist dealing with convalescents, the Catholic teacher is called upon to practice the arts which lead students to a full use of the Gift of Counsel and the virtue of prudence. Students must be encouraged to consult an instructor as they would consult a doctor. And they must be shown how to cure themselves: first, through a frank and humble diagnosis of their deficiencies, and then through an application of the special methods of self-therapy required by these deficiencies—which are psychophysical and even hygienic as often as they are intellectual. How to overcome awkwardness, how to control emotions, how to discipline nerves, how to avoid tension and make the fullest use of talent: these are the abilities, and others like them, which every teacher—not merely deans and advisers—must try to develop in all his students.

Every Catholic teacher must be, then, in the literal sense of the word, a psychiatrist, a Christian healer of the soul— a fact which is hinted at by St. Thomas when, in his superb article, "Whether one man can teach another," he points out that the work of the teacher is analogous to that of the medical doctor. Specifically, this requirement means that the teacher must be well-trained in diagnosing the symptoms of disintegrity—the symptoms of mental, emotional, moral, as well as spiritual, disease. He must be able to win the confidence and trust of the student and to suggest remedies so subtly and diplomatically that the student never thinks of himself as a patient. Finally, he must always be able, when called upon, to "see the student through" his various difficulties with parents and authorities: he must be thought of by the student as a wise and sympathetic friend.

Now, it is obvious that if these are the true aspects under

which students and teachers are to be viewed in Catholic education, all the other factors of that education must be determined accordingly—from the textbooks to the pictures in the corridors. But suffice it to say here that if what has been stated thus far is sound, the task of Catholic education can be summarized as that of aiding students to live and act as full Christians; that is, as dedicated, scientific artists, sound and heroic in the prosecuting of their vocations as members of the Mystical Body, and hence, as, in their way, priests, prophets and kings maintaining and perfecting civilization and bringing all things to a head in Christ.

Now, if it be objected at this point that what I have been describing is, though idealistic and interesting, still quite mistaken, the college being a place, after all, for the cultivation of the intellectual virtues alone, the reply can be made in the form of three questions. The first question is, what are these intellectual virtues, unless they be those mentioned by St. Thomas, wisdom, understanding, knowledge, prudence, and art, and which of them would the system of training I propose fail to cultivate? Second, if man was deprived of integrity through the loss of sanctity, may it not be well for us, even as an educational measure, to promote the restoration of integrity (as far as that may now be done) by helping him to regain sanctity, especially in view of the fact that the Encyclical on the Christian Education of Youth points to the saints as our best models? And, third, have we a right to take a young man away from the three most important educational institutions, the workshop, the home, and the parish, for four years and not give him something better than the training these institutions afford, especially in view of the fact that this same Encyclical emphasizes the necessity for educating the whole man?

The answers to these questions seem to me obvious and

IX

The Mastering of a Liberal Art

EASY as it may be for many people to accept the theory of "professional" training that has been touched on in the course of this book, it may not be equally easy for them to realize how different in certain ways this theory is, both in itself and in its implications, from the one to which they are used and which they more or less take for granted.

For that reason, it may be well for us to consider, at this point, just what is commonly meant today by the teaching of the liberal arts and then go on to note the difference between that concept of teaching and the concept that is suggested here.

When people speak of Liberal Arts education today, they generally have in mind some such notions concerning its purposes, objectives, methods, and motivation as the following:— It has for its end the turning out of cultured gentlemen, intelligent members of society, wise and urbane citizens of the world. To attain this end, it proposes to train the intellectual virtues, to stock the minds of students with basic knowledge of the various fundamental sciences, and to transform them into scholars, with a passionate love for the truth. The gaining of these objectives implies that each subject is to be dealt with as a science—as a carefully marked out and methodically organized body of tested knowledge about some one object or aspect of nature, an autonomous discipline, the purity of which is to be maintained carefully by a scrupulous regard for its own point of view, formal object, and methodology. As a subject for study, it is to be arranged and divided into units determined with reference to its natural articulation, the necessity for "covering the ground," and the capacity of the average student to absorb a given number of lessons through regular study (that is, of course, mainly through memorizing). The instructing is largely to be done through lectures, textbooks, reference works, visual aids, and demonstrations. That the student may make the information his own and be able to mark his progress for himself, as well as for others, he is, of course, called upon to recite, turn in reports, perform experiments, and pass examination. To assure the desired morale, the teacher must try to awaken the student's natural curiosity, stir him to unusual efforts through competition, give him a taste for the better things of life, and inspire him with an interest in his community.

Now, unfortunately, this theory, as a whole and in every one of its tenets, is not only inadequate, but delusive. Certainly it can hardly be said to be in accord with either the pre-Christian or the Christian theories of Liberal Arts education.

The object of turning out intelligent members of society, for instance, is inadequate. Athens, Berlin, Tokio—to mention only a few great centres of culture—all had thousands of intelligent members of society, cultured gentlemen, citizens of the world. Obviously, something more is needed.

Again, to train the intellectual virtues is excellent—but only on certain conditions. One is, that you do not make the mistake of assuming that knowledge is power; for, as St. Thomas carefully states, "scientia non est qualitas activa." Another is that you do not make the mistake of assuming that a knowledge of essences is the only essential knowledge. It is not even so in scholarship as Newman points out very strikingly in his work, *The Grammar of Assent*. Then, too, there is here the danger of assuming that practicality and utilitarianism are the same; and that, this being so, any study that is at all practical is necessarily illiberal and anti-intellectual; consequently, the best training for the intellect is that afforded by subjects which are of little or no use. Along with this absurd assumption goes another to the effect that there is no intellectual training in the practice of an art, but only in the discussion of it. The misconceiving and over-prizing of the intellectual virtues has even brought some theorists to deny the very existence of one of the intellectual powers, the cogitative sense, which is nothing else, according to St. Thomas, than the passive intellect itself.

As for stocking the student's mind with knowledge of many basic sciences, one can only say that it is a little naive to suppose that the student will thereby be enabled to recall the appropriate facts at need or to hit instinctively on the principle in accordance with which he is to evaluate, correlate, and apply his knowledge in solving a given concrete problem. Knowing all there is to know about an action is not the same thing as knowing how to do it.

Again, unless you understand very clearly what you mean by awakening a student's curiosity and inspiring him with a love for the truth, you may either fail or lead him into sin. You may fail simply through not realizing that man has very little love for truth itself; mostly, he loves the splendor of truth; that is, beauty. Unless, therefore, through recognizing the beauty of what you teach, yourself, and through showing your deep and wondering appreciation of it, you awaken your student to a similar delight in it and relish for it, you cannot expect to inspire in him anything like a love for it. The mind has to be trained to look for beauty—for the splendor of truth —just as certainly as it has to be trained to recognize the truth. And that there is grave danger in rousing the student's curiosity rather than his studiousness, that you may thereby be leading him into the sin of mental gluttony, is obvious.

Again, if by training the student to be a scholar, you mean training him to be scholarly whenever scholarship is required, that is one thing, and, of course, a good thing. But if you mean training him merely to rediscover, paraphrase, and compile the thoughts of others accurately, that is something else. Granted that every student should have this kind of training and that many students need it very much indeed, there is still a question whether it can be considered the highest or the principal form of training to be given in a Liberal Arts college.

If these commonly accepted purposes and objectives are questionable, so are the theories and the methods followed in achieving them.

That one science should not be taught as another is, of course, desirable. Students should not be taught to apply to one subject-matter the methods valid only for another. The lines of demarcation between science and philosophy must be drawn. Every science has its own general pattern. All these, admittedly, are truths to be respected. But in respecting them, we must be equally careful to avoid the danger of believing that there is such a thing as a "system," in the strict sense, of either philosophy or science; that somehow or other the textbook writers have discovered the kinds and relationships of the ideas in God's mind when he created the physical, moral, and sacramental orders; and that it is better to see things steadily than it is to see them whole, the ability to make distinctions being far more important than the ability to make syntheses, as if we did not proceed *componendo*, but only *dividendo*. A preoccupation with distinctions can also blind us to the fact that although the scientist must, as a scientist, stay within his own fields, the teacher of science is, of necessity, obliged not to do so.[1] The teacher who does not help his students correlate the given science with other cognate sciences, with metaphysics, and with Wisdom, is simply a poor teacher. Exactitude is important; but even more important is profundity.

The apparently scientific method of analyzing, or atomizing, the subject-matter of a science into neat little subdivisions is also questionable. Convenient as it may be for the investigator or for the teacher who feels under the compulsion of "covering the ground," it is dangerous in that it may accustom the student to an unsound way of studying. Who among those who ask students to follow this method would themselves, on taking up a new subject, use no more than one textbook of it and study this, one passage at a time, with ox-like regularity, day in and day out. Would they not rather assemble several classic, standard works on the subject and read these through until they had acquired some familiarity with the whole field, and then go back and take up one large division of it at a time, learning more and more every minute, but consciously memorizing almost nothing except a few conveniently phrased statements of principles, or a few vital tables of facts and formulae. This being so, why should we permit our students to indulge in the unsound practices of studying parts before wholes and of memorizing instead of familiarizing? Surely that theory is mere scientism, and therefore dangerously questionable, which holds that all things, the sciences included, are but aggregates of their parts, and that learning is the process of "adding" to one's knowledge.

The adoption of the pedagogical method derived from this theory, the method of lecturing, of demonstrating on the blackboard, of guiding students through the "performance" of experiments, can be similarly unfortunate, since it can suggest

[1] See Appendix D for a further treatment of this point.

that learning is a passive, rather than an active process, failing, as it does, to convince the student that he must produce his own knowledge, and suggesting that the main blocks to learning are mnemonic and intellectual rather than cogitative, emotional, and moral.

In line with this delusion is the further one, confirmed by our systems of testing, that what is of first importance is not anything else than the mere *reproduction* of knowledge. The recitation, the report, the test—all these can, to be sure, be useful; but unless they are managed very wisely indeed, they can do far greater harm than good. They can all too easily convince the student that the one thing that matters is the ability to recall the facts. What point is there in training oneself to evaluate, correlate, and make fruitful use of the facts in the solving of practical and theoretical problems when one is never to be tested closely on one's ability to perform these operations skillfully?

Nor is the theory we have been examining any less questionable in the motivation it proposes than in its objectives and methods; the motivation it proposes is, indeed, the worst thing about it. Regardless of the fact that curiosity, competition, and the love of intellectual luxury were, as St. Bonaventure points out in his *Breviloquium*, the three main motives whereby Satan caused the downfall of Eve, they are unacceptable even on purely technical grounds. The ambiguous form of curiosity here proposed, for example, can produce the antiquarian and intellectual gossip just as quickly as it can produce the historian or the teacher. And the motive of competition is so foreign to the spirit of true science or invention or the professions that it is simply not thought of by men in these fields: imagine Einstein hurrying to develop his theory, in fear that Abbé Lemaître would spring it first; imagine Edison trying to out-invent Westinghouse or Tesla or Hammond; imagine any doctor trying to monopolize medicine with a chain of hospitals. The motive, "the love of the better things of life," is, of course, sound enough—always provided that it does not mean merely the persuading of students to pass from a lower form of gluttony to a higher, or from a crude escapism to a refined. The real test of an education on this count is whether it is more of a punishment for students to give up their work—as it would be for a priest, a teacher, a poet, a doctor, an inventor, et al.—than it is for them to give up their pleasures and intellectual recreations. There is also the danger that "awakening in students the love for the better things" may come finally to mean narrowing their appreciativeness of all things: through concentrating their attention on a few products of the fine arts causing them to disregard the beauty of the products of all the other arts and even of God's handiwork itself.

Of the motive of humanitarianism, which is what, too often, is meant by "taking an interest in one's community," little need be said here, except, perhaps, that it can prove so plausible a substitute for true Christian Charity as to deceive even the elect.

The causes of all these educational delusions are many, but principally, I should say, the following:—1) Man's natural intellectuality, which causes him to cherish unduly the abstract and the essential at the cost of the concrete and the substantial; 2) man's natural desire for certitude (quiet of mind) which causes him to overprize exactness and precision and breadth of factual knowledge; 3) man's passionate hunger for the Beatific Vision, which causes him to become blindly infatuated with the mirages of it which he finds on earth: the love-affair; the fascination with science; the aesthetic experience; 4) his sheer laziness, which prompts him to rationalize his delight in formulae and to ignore the fact that knowing how a thing is done is not the same as knowing how to do it; 5) modern man's undue estimate of quantity, which causes him to treat wholes as if they were totals, mechanical division as if it were the only kind, and large amounts as inevitably more important than small—quality, intensity, and growth, all being sacrificed; 6) modern man's false notion of the effects of Original Sin, which, being thought to be mainly the harming of the individual faculties, rather than of their cooperativeness, are to be remedied by assuring the separate virtues of the separate powers through appropriate mental calisthenics —the cooperation of these powers naturally taking care of itself (much as the fortuitous concourse of atoms produces the whole ordered cosmos); and 7) modern man's failure to regard young men and women as anything but children; hence, his failure to train them in complete and responsible actions.

It should be clear, then, that the test of whether anything is an art—or of the extent to which it is an art—is very simple: has it to do with skill in making things or performances, and how directly has it to do with this skill? If a course in Biology, for instance, trains a student in investigating and dealing properly with living creatures, in themselves and as related to other creatures, to civilization, and to their Creator, it is an arts course; if it gives the student only a fund of accurate, well-organized knowledge about things animate, it is a science pure and simple. And so for all other courses in a college curriculum.

So much, then, for what is meant by the word, "art"; what are we to say is meant by the word, "liberal"?

If we go back to what seems to be its earliest use in Aristotle, we find that it refers to the state of the free man as against that of the slave; it refers, that is, to the man who was economically, as well as politically, free enough to have the leisure (The Greek word from which we get our word, "school," means, of course, "leisure") for scientifically mastering the arts he needed—with a full and profound study of their basis in the laws of nature. Not having to make money or get immediate results, the free man could take time for full study, usually forming an academy with his fellows to investigate the universal, philosophic principles in the light of which men could learn to prosecute the various arts of civilization so as to achieve happiness.

The word "liberal," then, properly refers to two things: the kind of subject studied and the way in which it is studied. The liberal arts consist of the kinds of arts which the free citizens of a country were to prosecute in establishing and conducting a civilization which leads to the happiness of its members. Thus, all free men needed to know how to debate and deliberate, how to reach a sound political decision, how to conduct themselves honorably, how to communicate eloquently, how to compose literary works like plays, how to discuss and philosophize, how to contemplate. Hence we find Plato and Aristotle composing masterly manuals of these arts: works so different from the kind of cut-and-dried science textbooks with which we are acquainted that we are liable to forget that these were the textbooks of the ancient world and, to a great extent, of the mediaeval. So practical and even technical a writing as the *Poetics*, for example, could still be considered by its author truly liberal because anything was truly liberal which could aid a free citizen to realize himself fully in a society he ran and perfected for that purpose: the full man being made by both the making of the society which enabled him to exercise his highest powers and by the intense exercise of these powers in the philosophic discussions of the symposia, or in the aesthetic meditation and purification afforded by the drama.

But even profound and vital arts can be studied illiberally: the term "liberal" referring, as I have said, not only to the kind but also to the depth of a study. That art alone is liberal in spirit which is studied with leisure, without worry, disinterestedly, in search of fundamental and ultimate principles, as if for itself alone—in much the same spirit, Cardinal Newman points out, as that in which a game is mastered. So it is that a subject which is, in kind, liberal can be made illiberal through the method by which, or the spirit in which, it is studied—as when, with hurry and worry, it is gone into superficially for the sake of immediate, personal, utilitarian gain—about as a stockbroker might learn botany or agriculture, the better to be able to deal in wheat on the grain market. And on the other hand, a subject like *Aerodynamics*, which could hardly be called a vital liberal art, can be studied liberally by men who seldom see a flying field and have no desire to do so. To be truly liberal, then, an art must be not only essential to assure the happiness of civilized men, but it must also be studied in the only way that is finally effective—in a spirit of liberal leisure.

On these points, I think, the Catholic Liberal Arts college is in agreement with the Academies of Plato and of Aristotle; the difference between it and them arises from the fact that the Christian has a fuller view of all things than has the greatest of pagans. The Christian agrees that any Liberal Arts College must be one in which the students are to master *arts* and to master them liberally, becoming scientifically and philosophically grounded artists. But he would go on to add that the Christian college must be something more than what is suggested by these words, "Liberal Arts": it must have a higher motive than they suggest, a wider range of arts to be studied, and a deeper spirit in which they are to be mastered. Since the Christian sees that the pagan chose to master the arts that lead to happiness on earth, there being, for the pagan, no vivid hope of any other kind, the Christian sees that the pagan really named his arts by an accidental quality—that they should have been called the Beatific Arts. Adopting a similar end to that adopted by the pagan, therefore, but with a full realization that man belongs, first of all, to a spiritual state, the Mystical Body, the Christian sees that man must be taught spiritual liberal arts as well as secular: that he must be made a freeman of the Kingdom of God, which includes earth, Purgatory and Heaven. And the liberality, the leisure and depth, of the educational process whereby man is to be made so must likewise be greater by far than any hoped for by the pagan; this, for three reasons: 1) because the principles on which the Christian is to found his skill stretch into the depths of God Himself; 2) because he needs the deepest freedom and peace for growing into an appreciation of these, making them part of himself; and 3) because he can feel free to take his time and acquire spiritual skill, being assured that without this he will never have the quality of leisure required for either the wisest use of other kinds of skill or even the full development of them.

We can come to a notion, therefore, of the kind of training we should be aiming at giving and hence to a notion of the methods implied by this kind of training, if we visualize the state we should have attained on becoming a true master of a Liberal Art.

Obviously, it is a state in which we should be expert both in prosecuting this art as an art and in developing and appreciating it as a science. It would be a state in which, whenever we found ourselves in a situation properly to be dealt with from the point of view, and by the special methods, of this art, we should at once recognize this fact, and immediately adopt that point of view and make skillful use of those methods: in the light of them, defining the problem exactly; identifying, with precision, its various factors; imaginatively and yet sensibly sketching out appropriate designs or hypotheses; ignoring extraneous considerations and bringing to bear quickly the universal principles that were pertinent; by scientific experimentation (real or imaginative) discovering new principles as required; recalling experiences of solving similar problems, as well as the theories and performances of past masters; making tactful, rather than servile, use of this knowledge; and working to a fresh final solution systematically, with much checking and revision, while employing throughout the dexterity which was the result of long practice in orderly methods. We should also like to be masters of the science of the art as a science, discerning clearly its distinctive realm of discourse: its formal object, its phenomena, its method, its criteriology, and its central laws; knowing them so well that we could give, off-hand, a sound, well-ordered, logical exposition of them.

To feel sure of arriving at this state of true mastery, we should undoubtedly wish to undergo some such training as the following:—First, we should like to become an understudy or aide to some already practising master of the art, being granted the privilege, under his general guidance, of taking on more and more difficult tasks, solving more and more complex problems, with fewer and fewer directions. Ideally, we should like to have these problems raised for us in systematic order; so that, with each new set of them, we should come to master a new division or level of the art, be required to have recourse to a new master principle, and be called upon to attain a fuller and more graceful technique. Meanwhile, we should like to have personal coaching that would facilitate the development of our skill both in performing whole and in experimenting to discover new principles for ourselves. Moreover, we should like to indulge in sessions of highly theoretical shop-talk, conducted Socratically; we should like to work out and appreciate theories actively which we might otherwise adopt passively. Further, once we had tried to work out each principle on our own, we should like to know exactly what the great performers and thinkers of the past had said and done, determining these things with the accuracy of a scholar, and then revise our performances and ideas in the light of theirs. Naturally, we should also like to be tutored in the science of the art considered as being an ordered body of tested knowledge and as bearing certain relations to other such bodies of knowledge. In short, we should like to have a training that consisted of a complex of apprenticeships, being: an apprenticeship in executing assignments under a master performer; an apprenticeship in dialectical (Socratic) discussion of the theoretical principles raised by the problems encountered in executing these assignments; an apprenticeship in the scientific methods required for perfecting the technique involved; an apprenticeship in the scholarly investigation and explication required for making the best (the soundest and most discriminating) use of the wisdom of the past.

To make all this clear by a concrete case:—Let us suppose that, having had your training in the arts of Logic, Cosmology, Psychology and Ethics, you wish to go and master the art of thinking and dealing with things metaphysically or ontologically. You therefore put yourself under a master of Metaphysics as an apprentice in this art. His first assignment to you runs as follows: "Will you kindly help me with the answer to a letter which I have just received this morning. You are not to consult any books or your memories of them: I am anxious to have you think the problem out freshly, on your own; this, for two reasons: I want you to get practice in independent thinking, and I want also to determine from your answer and from the answers of your fellow students how best to plan this course so as to meet your common needs accurately." He then presents a letter which reads in part:—

"I am now a member of our diplomatic corps stationed in Japan and very much concerned with the problem of how a conquering nation should deal with a conquered. Since I believe that no problem is ever solved solely on its lowest or on its intermediate levels, but on the highest as well, I should appreciate it greatly if you would give me your idea not so much of the Logical or Psychological or Ethical considerations governing our treatment of Japan as the purely Metaphysical. I regret very much that I did not have the privilege of studying under you, for I am told that you consider Metaphysics to be practically, as well as speculatively, valuable.

Very truly yours,
JOSEPH DOAKES

P.S. You may be interested to know that I am writing a similar letter to this to the head of the Religion courses, Fr. ———."

When you have read the letter, the Professor says helpfully, "I suggest that you keep in mind at least two principles here: 'Omne agens agit sibi simile,' and 'Quicquid recipitur in modo recipientis recipitur.'" Then, some time later, when you have performed the assignment, really trying to save your instructor some headaches by at least rehearsing the problem and blocking out a tactful reply for him, you and your fellow-students come together, and, under his guidance, hold a Socratic dialogue on the subject. Thereafter, he assigns the reading of certain passages in *The Republic*, in *The Politics*, in *The City of God*, and in the *De Regimine Principum*, as well as passages from other works which treat especially of the two principles which he suggested as central. At your next meeting, he gives a scholarly and primarily metaphysical *explication des textes* of these passages. And finally, he asks you to rewrite your letter in the light of the knowledge and by virtue of the skill you have now acquired, and also to phrase a compact exposition of what you have learned about efficient causality in itself, in its relations to the other causes, and in its bearings on politics, ethics, and theology.

Now, as far as possible, it is multifold training of this kind which the teacher of the liberal art is supposed to be giving to his students. Presumably, having had at least the equivalent of an interneship in his chosen art, he knows how to set realistic assignments in it that are also crucial instances: assignments carefully arranged and graded so as to require greater and greater skill, as well as involve deeper and deeper principles. He also knows how, as occasion demands, to guide his students into learning their theory for themselves, through sound experimentation and Socratic discussion. Further, he is thoroughly familiar with the science of his art, as he is likewise master of the pedagogical methods (including those of the dramatist and the writer of feature articles) which best enable his students, not only to absorb and correlate its findings, but also to think accurately, as scientists, in that field and yet broadly as philosophers and theologians, above and outside it.

All of which implies that the teacher of a liberal art must be *centrally* although by no means *solely*, concerned with the cogitative sense—the power which the positivist nowadays calls, somewhat crudely, intelligence. For, as we have seen, this is the power by which a person facing a whole, real situation judges instinctively and yet reasonably both what it means to him and what he should do about it. To give it an ordinary description, it is the power of the sound hunch— the most familiar form of which is, perhaps, what is usually called "feminine intuition," although all men have it too, however poorly they sometimes use it in matters social. It is, in fact, an intellectualized—at best, a spiritualized—form of the estimative sense. Just as an animal, in any vital situation, feels this situation to be for him or against him and thereupon feels the impulse to avoid what is bad there and to attain what is good, going on to choose, by a *sense* of their suitableness, the right means and methods for attaining his ends, so does man, when faced with a whole, real situation of importance to him, instinctively know it as both a real thing and a problem, and then go on to make an intellectual guess which he feels may be right, a working-hypothesis about the best means and methods for dealing with the situation successfully. Through the cogitative sense, man is able to see the concrete situation confronting him, not simply as a particular one, but also as a *case*, a *species*, a member of a class to which certain general laws apply and hence something to be dealt with by certain general methods which are determined by these laws. And under the feelingful guidance of this sense, he can then go on to guess which of these laws are of most consequence and which methods it will probably be *best* to invent or adopt. The cogitative, being at its lower end a sense, a faculty that feels the impact of the situation as concrete and peculiar, and, at its upper, nothing else than the passive intellect, which regards the situation as abstract and universal, is thus able to hand over to the active intellect, for experimental testing and ratiocination, the sound hunch to which it has reasonably "sensed" its way; so that, when the active intellect has worked upon this hunch, the possible intellect is able to see clearly, "in a flash," the exact nature of the situation and of the answer to it. A primary vague intuition becomes in this way the final clear intuition that is insight. To summarize, then, the cogitative sense, being the link between the spiritual and the sensitive—between intellect-and-will above and sense-and-impulse below—is a power *naturaliter Christiana*—one which enables us to know, to feel the impact of, all things as, in their way, minor incarnations; a power that enables us to deal with things as both physical and metaphysical, as creatures and as imitations of the ideas in the Mind of God (created ectypes of Christ) and subject therefore to metaphysical and spiritual laws.

Inasmuch as this sense as we shall see in the next chapter has been dealt with authoritatively by St. Thomas, by Péghaire,[2] and, though in a limited way, by Newman, I shall not enter into a further description of it here, except to indicate the conditions favorable to its development. These are: that the situations which the student is made to confront must be real; that they must "mean" enough to him to make him want to do something—not necessarily utilitarian, but something practical—about them; that they must be rich enough to engage, even a little distractingly—all his powers, as do good mathematical problems or puzzles; that they must be crucial enough to require deep thinking, that is, experimentation or ratiocination concerned with central principles; that they must be so arranged as to involve these main principles over and over again in *subtle* ways; that they must require a *quick, tentative solution before a careful, revised* one is worked out. Moreover, the student must be required always to clarify his intentions very carefully before executing them, and, above all, to be able to state the immediate and ultimate purposes of every action he performs; this, for the reason that technique follows intention. Ideally, to aid him in the transfer of skill as he goes from one art to another, he should have, I think, very early in his career, a course in the principles common to all artistic—that is, skillful—action—such a course as is outlined in another chapter. But whether he receives

[2] See bibliography 3, Appendix E.

such a course or not, he must at least be made aware of the fact that it is much more important for him to become a potentially great scientific artist than it is for him to become an actually great connoisseur or a "brilliant student."

All of which sounds very difficult—as does every form of brain treatment. It sounds especially difficult in a time in which the whole profession of teaching has reached such a low level that we do not expect every member of it to be as good as every member of any other profession. (How many— even of our teachers, to say nothing of parents—would expect our kindergarten teachers to have a training equivalent to that of our pediatricians?) But if the art of developing skill is so much more difficult than that of training memories that we simply must relinquish all hope of mastering this art, of prosecuting it, and of maintaining professional training in it, then let us at least give up the pretense of doing these things. Let us call our colleges honestly by a name that befits them: let us call them, not colleges of liberal arts, but colleges of letters and sciences.

That no such necessity faces us, however, that the art of developing skill is not impossible for any good mind to acquire, is being suggested and proved daily: it is being suggested by the way in which special tests have been supplanted by aptitude, intelligence, and ability tests; and it is being proved by the success of our various athletic coaches and our teachers of Medicine, as it has more than once been proved by our military men, who, having had to take as apprentices as unmilitary a generation of young men as ever existed, have shown that they could train these, in a few short months, to become the respected opponents of a nation noted for its military science. Given the same kind of standards and methods in the liberal arts that we now have in the athletic and the professional, we shall find that we can produce the same kinds of results. We can produce young men and women who are artists in all they do, making things that are full expressions of Charity through being full expressions of skill.

X

The Cultivation of Practicality

IF WE analyze carefully the general plan of education that
we have been considering, we shall see that it implies something more than sound training in the various liberal arts,
even what would ordinarily be called sound professional training; it implies a training that will meet one of the commonest
complaints lodged against the education which we are providing in our colleges today, the complaint that this education
is simply not practical enough. The man of business tells us:
"I just can't understand it. The young men we are hiring
these days seem not to know how to do anything. They don't
know typing, or bookkeeping—or anything else that is useful,
so far as I can see. They can tell you something about the
Wars of the Roses or the rhyme-scheme of a sonnet; but that's
about the only kind of thing they do know; and it's only
the teacher who can make any money out of that."

And, short-sighted as such an objector is, he nevertheless
has some right on his side. Every man who has had a college
education should be able to do any unfamiliar task better,
on the very first try, than he would have been able to do
it if he had not had a college education. Other things being
equal, a properly trained mind should always be able to turn
in a better performance than could that same mind left un-
trained. It is right that of two minds of equal strength and
experience the college-trained one should be uniformly the
more practical: the better able to get things done quickly and

efficiently. And I am afraid we must admit that at present it is not always able to do so.

But the remedies for this condition which the so-called practical man points out are hardly very practical. For usually, as we see in our public school systems, he calls upon us simply to add one more course to our curriculum: the course which supplies the particular need from which he is suffering at the moment—a course in Business English or in Accident Prevention or in Analysis of Propaganda or in the Russian Language or in Far-Eastern Problems. What he does not see is the futility of such a procedure: how the knowledge which he is asking students to acquire in the name of practicality may prove not at all practical when the momentary need for it has passed. Nor does he stop to consider how a course of secondary value may distract attention from another which, though less immediately engaging, is of primary and universal necessity. Again, he overlooks the dangers of dissipation of effort and the acquisition of a smattering of various kinds of knowledge. Seldom indeed has he any conception of the subtly demoralizing effect of his proposals on the minds of students: how the multiplication of special studies leads them to believe that a curriculum is a mere grab-bag of studies, all, so far as anyone really knows, about equally important; that education is a process of gaining a mere variety of equally important forms of skill; that because each subject is distinct from the other, not part of a carefully evaluated system, we can say there are methods, but no method. Students are thus made dependent on the masters of the "how-to" courses. They end by feeling that unless they have insured themselves against the chanciness of the modern world by the acquisition of a vast number of particularized forms of training, and unless they do so during the four years of college when they can sit at the feet of specialists, they will fail to get a truly realistic, and so a truly practical education. How else would it be possible for them to feel when they find that the very titles of their textbooks imply these attitudes (Business English; Mathematics for Today; American Rhetoric) and when certain college catalogues seem to list every kind of "how-to" course except that of How to Resist Magazine Salesmen Who Want Votes to Get Them Through College. The deadliest effect of all this is perhaps that of convincing the students that unless they get their education during their college careers, they will never get it: since all subjects are specialistic; since there are no general subjects on the basis of which one can, in later life, continue to educate oneself—then, obviously, the only thing to do is get the specialistic training when one can, and, at the same time, give up hope of filling out, on one's own, the scaffolding of a general culture. The best one can expect is to add, now and again, a new get-culture-quick course to one's collection.

In short, although the so-called practical man cannot be censured for asking of us that we turn out students well-equipped for action, he is not to be taken very seriously as an educator.

Nor is his somewhat more intellectual brother whose complaint usually runs about as follows: "The trouble with our students is that when they leave college, they are no better off than most when it comes to attacking a problem scientifically. What they need is more scientific training."

Here again, even if we are willing to admit, in the face of facts or for the sake of argument, that our students are not as practical, in the best sense of the word, as they should be, we may not be willing to admit that they will become so merely by undergoing more scientific training. To grant that our students are not very practical *and* that they are not very well trained in scientific method is not to grant that they are not very practical *merely because* they are not trained in scientific method. It is not to grant that mastery of a variety of scientific methods will, of itself alone, develop either inventiveness or facility; or that this will be done by *the* scientific method as such (express courses in which are given, so far as I know, in very few of our colleges).

Training in the special method of each science—and the special method of his own science is the only one in which the typical science teacher is likely to be interested—is almost certainly useful for that science alone or, or least, very difficult for most students to generalize and apply safely elsewhere. The student who knows how to analyze rubber, so as to discover whether it is natural or synthetic, does not necessarily know how to apply what is universally valid in this method to the analysis of two apparently similar cases in economics or politics or sociology. The "scientifically trained" student may become capable of attacking a variety of problems in a variety of sciences; he does not necessarily become capable of attacking any and every problem scientifically.

Nor would a course in scientific method as such give him, of itself, the key for which he was hunting—the key to *inventive* practicality. For whereas the scientist (who need not be a great inventor) is concerned with taking things apart to see what makes them tick and to measure that tick metronomically (or, if you prefer, with a Geiger counter), the inventor (who need not be a great scientist) is concerned with putting things together so that they will click as desired. Whereas the scientist sees a thing as a kind of realized conceptual entity, the inventor sees it as a substance that is an instrument: the chemist, for example, sees a silver spoon as a solid chemical; the silversmith sees it as a silver instrument for dipping and stirring. The chemist analyzes it for what chemical qualities it manifests and then for what one cause there is for each one of these qualities. The silversmith sees it as something determined by the needs of its user, by its material, by its pattern, and by the instruments that worked on that material. One sees it as a manifestation of certain principles, which can be dealt with separately and abstractly; the other sees it as a concrete combination of causes which produce one thing that satisfies a complex of needs. The one analyzes and formulates to enable us to understand theoretically; the other synthesizes and fashions to enable us to use practically.

Moreover, the scientist, once he has found out what is *generally* true of the aspects and elements of the things he is investigating, feels that his task is done. The inventor, on the other hand, looks upon the thing in front of him not merely as a general nature subject to various general laws (of chemistry, physics, psychology, ethics, etc.), but also as a concrete, particular nature requiring to be understood and dealt with (cogitatively) as such. The inventor must develop the habit of dealing with things synthetically, of responding to them as whole substances, of realizing them as *at once* universals and particular contingents, so as to come to grips with them *inventively*. And there is little in scientific training which, of itself at least, inevitably assures that the student will develop this habit.

Sometimes, in fact, what is called training in rigorous thinking, like that given in mathematics, is liable to unfit the student for realistic thinking. For example: if you ask most seniors in most of our colleges today—even those who should know better through having specialized in economics or logic—how long it would take four men to perform a task that takes two men a day to perform, you will receive the ridiculous answer, made almost automatically: "Why, half a day, of course." And if you ask them to stop and think for a minute to see whether they really mean what they have said, they look

at you as if you must be joking. Yet, as any practical fore-
man or sound philosopher knows, this answer is absurd.

For, the chance that men will ever act like mere machines, even when they are faced with the most mechanical
task, that chance is, thank God, negligible. As the theory of
holism, the fallacies of composition and distribution, and the
laws of increasing and diminishing returns should all warn the
student, the men will either cooperate efficiently or not; and
the conditions will be either favorable or not for the use of
four rather than of two men. But it is extremely unlikely that
they will be able merely to *add* or lump their efforts together
and do so uniformly, minute by minute. They will either get
the work done in much less than half the day or, perhaps,
fall to quarrelling over "who is lying down on the job" and
end up in a hospital. Rigorous thinking—so called—may be
usefully suggestive; but practically, there is danger in believing that it can deal adequately with a universe that, after all,
was not created by a committee of mathematicians.

Now what both the practical man and the proponent of
scientism—what in fact we should all really like is the educating of students in a method which would be 1) artistic and 2)
philosophic. They would like to have us train students to make
things or performances, not merely to analyze or to understand these, nor merely to make them with the *simplisme* of
the scientist. They want students made ready for each *new*
thing or performance through knowing the philosophic principles governing the making of *every* thing or performance.
What is called for here, then, is a course in the philosophy
of craftsmanship, or art.

As I have had occasion to point out elsewhere (see the
Chapter "Integration—Skill" in *The Idea of a Catholic College*) we are provided with the basic notions, the pattern,
and the methods of such a course by the Aristotelian-Thomis-

tic theory of causal analysis. For if it is true that every thing
or performance is the result of its four causes—its matter, its
form, its efficient cause, and its final cause—or, less technically,
its material, pattern, instrument and function—then, obviously, the assuring of these four causal factors duly means
the assuring of a well-made thing or performance.

Such a course would make easy the preliminary integrating of most of the other subjects which the student is to take
up, because from the outset he would, through it, be getting
the necessary but unrefined—the common sense—notions of
what he would later refine in each of his courses. He would
in this way be familiarized with many of the problems of these
courses. He would come to know these problems as real, and
feel the practical necessity for getting a full theoretical appreciation of them. His education would thus proceed from a
first-hand descriptive philosophizing to a purely causal philosophizing.

I say that this course would make easy the preliminary
integrating of the other courses in the curriculum because
"the course is based on the notion that it is desirable for
the student to consider ultimate as well as immediate, con-
cepts, axioms and principles. The student comes to see that to
know matter thoroughly, for instance, he must view it not
simply as the chemist or the physicist knows it, but also as
the cosmologist does. To understand thoroughly the main
instrument of all production, man, the student is compelled
to study him not merely as the psychologist does, but also
as the ethician and the metaphysician do. To appreciate the
factor of form properly, the student must know something of
the difference between image and concept, the particular and
the universal—hence, something of logic, epistemology: the
theories of criteriology that stem from Platonic Idealism,
Aristotelian Realism, Cartesianism, Pragmatism. To know the

factor of purpose thoroughly, he must have some understanding of the whole great argument about teleology—about the reality of Final Causes—as well as that of Functionalism in industrial Design and Architecture. Thus the student comes to see that all the philosophic disciplines have a direct bearing on his daily life."

Here I might also add that such a course as this would prove a valuable aid to the study of history. For through the making of any simple thing, the individual maker comes to understand what it is to arrive at an estimate of what is needed for someone's happiness, of the materials, instruments, methods, patterns and plans which are required ideally, of those that are available actually, of what can be done to bridge the gap between the ideal and the easy, of how fate takes a hand and "the best-laid schemes of mice and men gang aft agley," and so on. And, having realized such facts about the making by individuals of single, simple things, the student can begin to see in like terms the attempt of a great leader, of a group of pioneers, or of a nation to meet the needs of a certain way of life through transforming a new or an inherited environment and using the potential in men and in materials in accordance with a certain plan. Each new historical movement in mankind's attempt to establish a Utopia, another Garden of Eden, or the Kingdom of God on earth, will thus become clarified for them as a craftsmanly or artistic achievement. It will in this way be made a dramatic adventure and also an experiment. Through familiarity with the patterns and elements of successful and unsuccessful enterprises, the student will be enabled analogically to keep alive what our friends the Existentialists say we usually allow to atrophy—the sense of how things actually work out in the lives of individuals, societies and whole nations. In fact, since they will take up each of their courses as training for the making of history, in the fostering of the growth of the Kingdom of God, the students of a true course in the philosophy of craftsmanship will gain their sense of history from an apprenticeship designed to help them make history. They will gain a craftsman's sense of it, rather than a mere critic's.

This course should prove of great importance as integrative in another way also. For if all courses are properly to be mastered as arts, then it is clear that a course which trains students in the fundamental principles common to all the arts will enable these students to see their courses all as simply different species—as different exemplifications of the same general virtue. The result will be that, even if students never work out (and who at the present time has done so very surely?) a clear, comprehensive map of all the branches of knowledge, visualizing them as a system, they will nevertheless be able to feel their fundamental unity as arts and as at least ancillary to a unified plan for the restoration of all things in Christ.

The kind of course which I am suggesting here would ideally be ordered, I believe, somewhat as follows:

(1) There would be about one hour a week of theory, which would be worked out by Socratic discussion and summarizing lecture. At least two hours a week would be given to craft-workshop practice, in which special problems would be set involving the principles arrived at in the discussion period.

(2) During the first month, the students should practice general cursory analysis of relatively crude and simple things made in the workshop and commonly used in the home—clothespins, table-mats and the like.

(3) During the next period of the course, the students would design and analyze other simple things,

now paying special attention, however, to the factor of purpose.

(4) Next, they would do so paying special attention to purpose and material. And so, cumulatively, to purpose, material and form, to purpose, material, form and instrument.

(5) The course should cover thereafter the making of complex objects; then of machines; and then of organizations.

(6) In a final period, the course could become more classroom, less workshop: the instructor getting into the implications of its separate doctrines as these appear in, or determine, the making and redeeming of a civilization.

The difficulties which confront anyone who would initiate any such course as this are, it seems to me, these:—

1) There are very few teachers of the crafts who know enough about philosophy to use craftsmanship as the illustration or the practical manifestation of philosophic principles —and vice versa.

2) Moreover, there seem to be few teachers who are capable of making up the kind of Socratic method that is best suited to this sort of course. As an illustration of what I mean by a Socratic method, may I cite the following which would be read to a class and discussed with them example by example:—

Thought-Provoker on Form

1. A rheumatic geometry teacher draws a wavy, three-sided figure on the board and asks a pupil: "What is the form of this?" The pupil says that it is a drawing made up of three wavy lines that meet. The teacher gets angry, and

says: "These lines are not the form of what I am talking about; they are only the form of a *picture* of what I am talking about." Is the teacher right?

2. To prove his point, the teacher draws two similar pictures, one much larger, the other much smaller than the first. Then he asks: "Does it matter whether I use one or the other of these to prove a theorem?" The student answers: "No, all triangles are alike, no matter what size drawings you use." "Then," says the teacher, "the form of the triangle is not the same thing as the form of the drawing. What do you mean, therefore, by the 'form' of a triangle?" Well, what *do* we mean?

3. Someone says to an untutored Eskimo: "There are only a few fundamental forms: the circle, the triangle, the square. The rest are combinations of these." The Eskimo says: "That is very interesting. Which one of these is the hardest to destroy? Which will stand up best?" The other says: "The triangle, I should imagine." And the Eskimo asks: "Is, then, the democratic form of government a triangle?" What shall we say? That the word "form" cannot properly be used for government?

4. You hear a piece of music played on an ocarina or a flute and you go off whistling it. Have you captured the form of the piece you have just heard?

5. What definition could apply to the form of a triangle, to the form of the image of the triangle, to the form of a government and to the form of a piece of music?

3) And the third objection is that there are no textbooks on this subject, since it does not form a part of the traditional *corpus* of Scholastic philosophy. Many even deny the possibility of there being such a division of philosophy.

The possibility of this discipline, however, can be proved, I believe, by the following:—

Whether or not Technology is science

Objection 1. It would seem that Technology cannot be a true science because there can be no science about particulars. But all art, which is the subject-matter of Technology, is about particulars. Therefore Technology cannot be a science.

Objection 2. Moreover, if it is not about particulars, it must be about universals. But universals are dealt with exhaustively in the already established sciences. Therefore Technology cannot be a true science, but only a mass of information collected from already established sciences.

Objection 3. Furthermore, to assume that the mind can deal with the particular in a purely rational way is to assume the existence of a "ratio particularis," a particular reason. But there is no such thing as a "ratio particularis." Therefore, Technology cannot be a true science inasmuch as it requires the use of a power which does not exist.

But, on the other hand:—If it is possible for us to have a general science (Ethics) of one of the virtues of the practical intellect (prudence), it would seem possible for us to have a general science (Technology) of the other virtue of the practical intellect (art).

Conclusion: It is possible for Technology to be a science because, although it deals with particulars, it deals with them scientifically—that is, as particular instances of *universals*—by virtue of a faculty that is intermediate between sense and intellect (the cogitative sense, or passive intellect[1]).

[1] The cogitative sense and the passive intellect are the same. The passive intellect and the possible intellect are not the same. The cogitative sense has a right to be called a "ratio particularis." These are the beliefs of St. Thomas, as Julien Péghaire has shown in his brilliant article, "A Forgotten Sense, the Cogitative," in *The Modern Schoolman*, March and May, 1943, from which I take the liberty of citing these footnotes:

42 *Cf.* especially *Sum. c. Gent.* 11. 60 *passim*, 73 *passim*. These chapters should be quoted in their entirety. We shall quote only *In VI Ethic.*, lect. 9 (Pirotta ed.), n. 1249: ". . . vim cogitativam sive aestimativam

Proof: Here it must be said that there are two ways of dealing with the particular. One is that of the animal; the other is that
of man. The animal responds to a situation *estimatively;* man responds to it *cogitatively.*

Thus, to use a classic example, when a ewe sees a wolf, she
senses him as a colored object of a certain color, shape, size, etc.
But, although she senses him only as a particular thing, she receives a certain quasi-judicial impression of him—an impression of
his dangerousness to her. She also has a "sense" of whether it
would be better for her to stand her ground and fight or to flee,
and she flees.

So, too, a man who is confronted by another creature, whether
enemy or obstacle, friend or auxiliary, senses it as good or bad for
him and adopts the method of dealing with it that he "feels" is
right. But, unlike the ewe, a man senses an obstacle or an enemy,
not simply as a particular thing, but as an *instance* of a certain
kind of thing: he sees it not merely, let us say, as this one slippery
boulevard or this one gangster or this one fire, but also as this *instance* of a slippery boulevard, this *instance* of a gangster, this
instance of a fire. His feeling of its goodness or badness—his
"sense" of its dangerousness—is the result of his impression of it
as a concrete embodiment of a nature. And the conjecture that
he follows in dealing with it is not merely a sensory, but a sensory-
intellectual conjecture. His understanding of the general nature
of any such thing suggests to him, "gives him the feeling of,"
which *general* principles apply here and which do not, while his
sense of the uniqueness of the thing makes him feel what might
be the best *particular* actions to take in accordance with these

---

quae dicitur ratio particularis. Unde hic sensus vocatur intellectus qui est
circa sensibilia vel singularia. Et hunc Philosophus vocat in tertio *de
Anima* intellectum passivum, qui est corruptibilis."

43
　　Cf. among other passages: *In II Sent.,* d. 23, 2. 2. sol. 1 ad 3; *In
III Sent.,* d. 26, 1. 2; *In II de Anima,* lect. 13 (Pirotta ed.), n. 396;
In VI. Ethic., lect. 1, n. 1123; *In I Meta.,* lect. 1. n. 15; *Sum. c. Gent.,*
11. 60. n. 1; *Quaest. de An.,* art. 13; S. T., 1. 78, 4, and 1. 81. 3; *De
Potentiis Animae,* c. 4 (Mandonnet ed.), vol. V, p. 355.

principles. His conjecture (his "hunch") is an intellectual one: he adopts and follows a method based on, not a mere guess, but a *hypothesis* that he feels is sound.

Therefore, we can say that skillful action, artistic action, differs from instinctive in being both intellectual and sensory, both voluntary and impulsive, rather than sensory-impulsive alone. In skillful action man obeys impulses dictated by the felt sensory-intellectual impression of the object with which he is dealing. Consequently, the better he knows the general nature of every factor, as a factor, in any event of making, the more intellectual, scientific, and reliable will be his response to it, and the more discriminate will be his obedience to his so-called instinctive impulses.

General Technology is, then, a science in that it is concerned with the *general* nature of all the factors of any act of making, the general laws governing these factors individually and collectively, and the general principles in accordance with which the cogitative sense may be refined in obeying these laws.

To the First Objection: It may be said that General Technology does not deal with particulars primarily as particulars; it deals with them as special instances of the general act of skillful making or performing.

To the Second Objection: It may be said that although General Technology deals with universals, it deals with them in two special ways: first, as concerned with acts of skillful, efficient making; second, as unified in accordance with the requirements of cogitation. And since no other science has either this object or this ordering, General Technology has a right to be considered a science by itself.

To the Third Objection: It may be said that:—"Action is of the person." But the person cannot act either sensorily only or intellectually only. By his very nature (and by the requirements of it) the human being must and can deal with particulars-as-embodiments. In so doing, the person obeys, not merely the active intellect, which rectifies and tests, nor merely the possible intellect, which sees and assents to what the active intellect has worked on, but the passive intellect which presents the conjecture or the hypothesis that the active intellect works on. If we grant these facts, we grant the existence of the cogitative sense and the possibility of training it.[2]

A course of this kind is, therefore, possible, and can, I feel sure, be made even generally feasible. I myself have given something like it about three or four times, once with the aid of a teacher of design. And I am sure that it can be connected with any craft with which a teacher may be familiar; for example, with the craft of writing. Once, in fact, a student begins to grasp the notion of how a piece of writing is what it is—and not something else—because of its exact purpose, its subject-matter, its form and its writer's technique; once he sees every piece of writing as something the production of which was strictly determined by these four causes, he can also be shown the nature of these causes themselves and their interdependence through an analysis of various forms of writing. He can be taught the philosophy of making as manifested in the art of composing, just as he can be taught the art of composing as determined by the philosophy of making.

What is mainly required here is that teachers of philosophy take up some craft or range of crafts, and that craftsmen and teachers of crafts in turn take up philosophy with

[2] When we speak of "training the cogitative sense," or of training any other sense, for that matter, we are, of course, speaking inaccurately. The student of music who acquires the ability to distinguish chords is not training his sense of hearing, except insofar as the muscles and nerves of his ear are kept healthy through normal exercise. What he is really training is the intellect and the sense of hearing in the habit of adjusting themselves to one another; the intellect learns what qualities to listen for in a given chord (the variety and unity of its system of tones) and the sense learns to recognize and appreciate the chord as having this system of tones. Through knowing what *must* be, the student can best hear what *is*; it is by listening *for* certain tones that he best listens *to* them. Similarly, for the cogitative sense: it is by our showing it the qualities of the possible that we can train it to plan or visualize what is probable: it is by training it to imagine what *might* work that we can enable it to invent what *will* work.

the idea of applying to their crafts its doctrines on finality, materiality, efficient causality and formality. This venture would soon produce enough teachers of the philosophy of craftsmanship to meet our needs.

Meanwhile, almost any course in philosophy can be given Socratically, at least in part, even if we do no more than establish supervised discussions as laboratory periods. Almost any philosopher, moreover, should be able to do something for the development of a philosophy of craftsmanship, and do so without fear, since any course in this subject would be followed later by fuller and more exact formal courses in the various disciplines it implies—cosmology, psychology, ontology etc. This course could be to other disciplines what Platonism was to Aristotelianism, or what scholarly shop-talk is to the monographs and the technical journals dealing with the same subject.

At all events, I think that we must at least make up our minds on whether there is such a thing as a course dealing with art as such, or whether we must consider our curricula to consist of essentially diverse arts which can only be unified as sciences, and finally, whether we can integrate the techniques of these sciences in such a way as to meet the objections pointed out at the beginning of this chapter, the objections that our students graduate with no practical sense and no special ability to attack any and every problem methodically. For it is by answering these questions satisfactorily that we shall make our colleges true colleges of Liberal Arts.

XI

The Requirements of Morale-Building

WHEN we repeat after the Pope that education is meant to train the "whole man," we are all too prone to overlook the fact that part of the whole man is his nervous system. We are liable to ignore the fact that Original Sin has made it necessary for us to develop in our students a certain morale, without which they may not attain even the intellectual skill which they are supposed to attain.

No discussion of Catholic education would be complete, therefore, without a consideration of this necessity. For that reason, I shall try to deal with it in the present chapter as thoroughly as I can. And since this attempt will require a somewhat circuitous attack on the subject, I feel obliged, in fairness, to begin with a general outline of my points before I take them up in order.

These points may be summarized as follows:—

To perform any act of skill requires morale. Unless a man has confidence, inner peace, courage, love of perfection, enthusiasm, he will not perform his tasks as skillfully as he should. But, as a result of original and actual sin, no man is possessed of such virtues naturally. No man's powers work together easily and harmoniously. And it is now doubly difficult for him to make them do so inasmuch as other men, so-called leaders, have learned, for selfish reasons, how to rob him of his habits of self-control, luring him or hypnotizing him into doing their will impulsively and unthinkingly. Unconsciously, he is being "conditioned" to act not from the highest motives (the love of perfection and Charity) but from the lowest (pride, fear, and concupiscence). And the greatest art—or even good work—can never be produced by men so motivated. One of our principal tasks, therefore, as educators concerned with the development of skill is that of developing sound morale in our students. It is a twofold task: being, first, that of showing them what the tricks of demoralization are which they will have to resist and how to resist them; and, second, that of transforming them into young heroes and heroines who have the confidence and the enthusiasm necessary for acting as skillfully as possible in the great cause of establishing the Kingdom of God on earth.

The development of skill, in other words, is quite as much a matter of moral, as it is of intellectual, virtue. For, unless a man is trying to be a saint as a technician—unless, in his own work at least, he is a man of great virtue—he will simply not be as efficient as he should and can be. Whether he be a shoemaker or a poetic dramatist, unless he is charitable enough to think first of the good of his patron, he will produce something unsuitable, or he will pander and cheat, dazzling the eye while turning out something essentially shoddy. Unless he is humble, he will think first of "expressing himself"; that is, of fashioning something that will display his virtuosity rather than answer the needs of others; or he will turn out what is mannered rather than truly stylish. If he is proud, he will not be able to take useful criticism and put it to account. (Think of the improvements that could be made overnight in all our institutions and our techniques if all those in authority from the lowest to the highest could really welcome sound criticism!) If a maker is subject to avarice, he will turn out simply what makes money, cheapening, adulterating, "glamorizing," his product so as to trap the gullible, the stupid, and the greedy bargain-hunters.

If he is quick to anger, his very technique will suffer, for skill requires a cool head. If he is slothful, he will never finish his work properly. If he is lustful, he will be continually distracted by his evil fantasies and intrigues; and his brutalized imagination will favor ugly ends and patterns. If he is envious, he will think, not of what is best to be done, but only of how to do something a little different, a little more "original" and attractive than what his competitor is doing. And unless he has great fortitude, practising his art whole-heartedly, taking infinite pains, indefatigably revising, revising, revising, always holding himself to his highest standard of achievement, abhorring second-rate work as both unnatural and unworthy to be offered to God, he will never be the artist that he should be, no matter how many people form a cult of him and cherish him as a demigod.

The great secret, indeed, of the development in the Middle Ages of a technical skill that leaves us overwhelmed with admiration is that it was the fruit of sound spirituality that incidentally assured sound morale. Inspired by the doctrine and the examples of Charity given them by their great saints, the craftsmen of good will banded together to establish the conditions and institute the discipline best suited for making things, in every sense, rightly. Through the Mass and through devotions to a patron saint, they offered their work to God, as performed for the charitable alleviation of human needs. To make it satisfy, in justice and charity, the needs of all concerned, they formed associations for the maintenance of the highest possible quality, for the elimination of fear of competition, for the full and careful and spiritual training of apprentices, poor as well as rich, for the establishment of fair prices, for the care and consolation of needy fellow-craftsmen and their dependents, as well as of the poor in general—in short, for the guaranteeing of conditions in which a poor but good-willed and duly talented young man who wished to make a vocation of his craft could learn to work under a master artist, who was also required to act as foster-father, in an atmosphere of Christian fortitude, peace and Charity, the atmosphere ideal for the full development and use of his skill.

And even though this atmosphere was never quite assured in all its purity—or never for more than a short while, the Middle Ages, as it is well to remember, having never attained anything like a perfect Christendom—even so, the results were truly astounding. Moreover, if we look about us alertly in this our own day, we shall observe how true it still is that only when something like the conditions aimed at by the old Guildsmen are attained do we achieve technical advances worthy of the name. The Medical Associations of the world, half-blind as many of them are spiritually, and certainly no more than quasi-Christian, still demonstrate what a body of men can do who recognize morals to be a main determinant of art. And despite the claims of our industrialists that it is only the spirit of "enterprise" (more nearly, avarice) and competition (more nearly, envious fear and jealousy) which produce our mechanical advances, the truth is that these motives have little to do with such advances. These very industrialists do all that they can, in fact, to assure, in their laboratories of investigation and invention, as much freedom from commercialism and competition as possible. The present-day technical colleges and industrial laboratories are as close facsimiles to the medieval workshops as a pagan mind that has retained vestigial memories of a Christian civilization can make them; and this, for the very good reason that only by being so can they produce the best results.

It would seem fairly obvious, therefore, that it is only to the extent to which we turn out young artists (as the

medievals called their students) who have the right moral
disposition for their work that we are turning out persons who
assure the highest development, individual and communal, of
the various arts. Hence we shall do well here to study carefully what we have to deal with in trying to assure these
desirable moral dispositions: the source and nature of the
perverse tendencies in man; the conditions under which these
are provoked; how our principal enemy, Satan, tries to assure
these conditions; and then, what we can do to strengthen our
students in following our Divine Leader enthusiastically and
in going on to assure proper conditions, so that others also
may find it less difficult to become Christian artists like themselves.

Now, the evil tendencies in man, the tendencies which
destroy his morale and prevent the establishing of the conditions ideal for the prosecution of craftsmanship and art, are
directly traceable to man's having turned away from God in
original sin and to his continuing to do so in actual sin. For,
through his having turned away from God, man lost the inner
harmony, the light and the will-power required for the most
effective action. He could not, as it were, pull himself together and see things in their proper relation to the central
principle of the cosmos, God, but only in relation to this
or that combination of minor principles, creatures, or creaturely goods. And inasmuch as the most profound, the most
truly scientific, knowledge of things results from seeing them
in the light of their ultimate cause, and inasmuch as God *is*
that ultimate cause, man through losing contact with God,
first lost the gifts of knowing, appreciating, trusting and loving
Him duly (the virtues of Faith, Hope, and Charity), then the
infused virtues of prudence, justice, temperance, and fortitude, and finally, even ease in acquiring the natural forms of
these virtues (the ordinary maker of things having to struggle,

for instance, against such tendencies as that of being imprudent in the choice of materials, instruments, and patterns; unjust in disregarding his patron's needs and in forcing his materials and instruments; intemperate in his virtuosity, or in his commercialism, lacking in fortitude, as this is required for originating, completing, or perfecting). Finally, as we shall see, man's very psycho-physical habits have become affected: as we see in athletics, the very integration of the body with the mind being, often enough, a highly esteemed achievement.

The mechanism, or causal chain, for man's present state of disintegration would seem to be this:—When man has lost Faith, Hope, and Charity, he can no longer believe in his heart that there is for him a reward in another world, so that he then becomes extremely anxious to enjoy in this world as much security, as many creaturely goods, and as much inner peace as possible. As a consequence, he becomes intensely desirous, concupiscent: he desires to rejoice in his own power and to enjoy ease and the satisfaction of all his appetites. The concupiscible in him escapes governance by a will enlivened by grace working under the guidance of a reason illuminated by grace. Any technical method then seems to him desirable which gains for him the satisfaction of concupiscence, regardless of how little useful to the patron or how intrinsically defective his product may be. And the irascible becomes an equally grave source of bad craftsmanship. Overwhelmed by a passionate desire for quick and selfish results, a craftsman cannot help falling prey to the two extreme vices of irascibility. In the face of a stubborn difficulty (and to the impatient and impetuous all difficulties, even the simplest, will seem like personal affronts) he will do only one of two things: execute headlong the counsels of proud rage (presumption); or stumble about and fumble in trying to carry out those of bewildered fear (despair)—in either case his faculties being "stampeded" into an irrational act. Those actions which result mainly from concupiscence (from lust, sloth, gluttony, avarice) may therefore be considered to be negatively wrong, being mainly forms of non-feasance; whereas the actions which result from concupiscent irascibility seem positively wrong, being rather forms of misfeasance and malfeasance. For, under the influence of pride and anger, a craftsman acts in either a blind and awkward impetuousness or in a deceptive and spellbound cautiousness: rage rendering him subject to delusions and seductive suggestions.

There are, of course, other unfortunate disabilities than these, disabilities that are both psychopathic and hygienic, which likewise result from man's loss of grace and the virtues it assured and which render men poor craftsmen simply by crippling them. But since these effects have been dealt with fully and completely by such men as Dr. Rudolf Allers and Dom T. V. Moore, I shall limit myself here to a basic description of them. Certainly, it should not be too difficult for any of us to see that the man who gives up all reliance on God and tries to rely on himself alone, or even primarily, is always endangering his mental health. Such a man, devoid of Faith, Hope, and Charity, cannot help falling back on a strong belief in himself; for, after all, he is aware, however dimly, that he is in the image and likeness of God. And yet in conflict with this belief in his essential goodness, there grows up in him the equally strong belief, born of hard and bitter experience, that he is incapable of solving the problems of life or of doing anything skillfully enough to satisfy his own standards. Consequently, it is no wonder that, in trying to free himself of the complexes which result from this conflict of equal certitudes, he cripples himself by false forms of retreat, defense, compensation, and sublimation, making his craftsmanship subservient to the requirements of these actions of mal-adjustment, rather than to those of satisfying his patrons. And hygienically, his falling prey to passions also endangers his technique—simply through debilitating him. Often enough, the work of art which gains its effect surely differs from that which "almost comes off, but does not quite" for one reason only: the first has been executed by a man with a reserve of energy; the second has not. And since this precious reserve can be most quickly wasted through indulgence in passionate emotion (anger, anxiety, disgust, shame, remorse, hatred, etc.); since, in fact, one fit of rage can cost (as Aveling points out) as much energy as is used up in a day of manual labor, it is obvious to anyone who counts the sighs of this poor world just how disastrous for finesse of all kinds was the sin of Adam.

Pursuing these considerations no further, then, I shall confine myself here to a general exposition of how and why concupiscence and irascibility prove destructive of morale.

That the man who is "very even-tempered—always angry" is not likely to be a skillful performer is so well known that even the most moronic of prize-fighters always tries, as he poetically puts it, "to get the other guy's goat"—as did his ancient predecessors the Anglo-Saxon warrior champions, who made a practice of insulting their opponents eloquently before battle, for the same purpose. Long experience has shown that the hot-headed warrior soon becomes the cold-headed one, lying in the dust before the cool-headed.

We can see why this method is effective—and therefore how and why we must be able to deal with it in our commercial "battles" today—if we turn to the scientific explanation of some of the psycho-physical causes for its effectiveness as these have been worked out in the past few years by Dr. Cannon and his followers. Roughly, the effect of anger, according to Cannon's theory, is to awaken the adrenal glands, which then stimulate the body to prepare for violent actions of preservation: they cause the blood to be withdrawn from the higher brain centers, from the stomach—in fact, from those organs generally which are not concerned with effecting the desired action, inducing the blood also into those which are so concerned: the lower brain, the lungs, the arms, back, and legs. Briefly, the emotion stimulates the glands which tone up the body, preparing it for quick and violent movements of self-defense.

Now, for our purpose, the important thing to note here is that the action thus prepared for is *violent*; that is to say, hard, fast, and crude. It is not an action of *finesse*. This fact has been brought out in an experiment in which young men were stimulated by adrenalin and then given tasks to perform some of which required *finesse*, others of which did not. The last words of the report on the experiment run: "The results of the tests of the mental and motor performance showed that adrenalin did not favor mental efficiency, while the motor activities were somewhat improved by the drug."[1]

When we realize that the adrenal glands are set in action by fear as well as by anger, we are able to see still more clearly that in the disjoining, by original sin, of the irascible from the intellect and will and in the widening of this breach by the actual and habitual sins of presumption, anger, envy, jealousy, and despair, we have one of the main sources of impulsive, rattle-brained, heavy-handed, and clumsy action. And since great art of any kind requires cool, deliberate, dextrous, graceful thinking and executing, we can be sure that it is not the product of men who approach their work in a spirit of angry pride or jealous competition or fear of awkwardness or failure.

[1] *American Journal of Psychology*, July 1931, Vol. XLIII, pp. 447-56.

If only because of its psycho-physical effects, passionate motivation is inefficient.

Turning now to the conditions under which the irascible can be not so much overstimulated as paralyzed, taken captive, and misdirected into action that is positively wrong and foolish, we find that these conditions are, surprisingly enough, exactly those of what is known as hypnosis. Moreover, they are the very conditions which the military leader tries to assure when he tries to seduce his enemy into actions that are insane, self-thwarting, and disastrous.

For the master of military psychology knows that if he is to gain victory as economically as possible, he must try to trap his enemy into a bewildered misuse of his powers by frightening and hypnotizing him into following the wrong course of action and into an awkward prosecution of that course of action.

He knows, further, that he always has a good chance of thus demoralizing men since, men being what they are, it is usually possible either to shake their confidence in themselves and to throw them into a paralyzing state of inner confusion. Thus, he knows that if men are to act effectively in any difficult undertaking, whether it be fighting or not, they must be convinced that both their actions and the means they are employing are true, good, and beautiful—right, effective, glorious—and that in so acting they are showing themselves to be true men (not weaklings), good men (not monsters), beautiful men (that is, heroes, not bullies or glamorous brutes). The moment they are robbed of confidence in their cause, in their technique, in their instruments, in their leaders, in their fellows, and in themselves, they begin to fall prey to a vague fear which skillfully played upon, will make them act wildly and disastrously, following any course, however silly, that their seducers themselves may suggest to them.

The master of military psychology sees this opportunity as always open to him because he can rely on the following truths of human nature as certain:—

First, that every man may be, for practical purposes, regarded as a bundle of instincts, or a federation of minor selves. A man is either an army of faculties, well-disciplined and controlled by his will and reason, or he is a mob of faculties, ill-disciplined and controlled by his passions and impulses.

Second, that since it takes energy and will-power for him to discipline and control his faculties, it is easy for a man to be a mob and hard for him to be an army. It is only through good habits and reasoning that man assures the team play among his faculties which is necessary for unified, coordinated, and hence skillful action. Consequently, it is easy to stage a revolution among them, so that the legitimate powers of reason and will can be dethroned and some usurping set of instincts or habits take over.

Third, that this dethroning and usurping can be accomplished by the assuring of a hypnotic condition in which, the higher powers having been lulled to sleep, a minor self takes over, as it were, and acts impulsively and blindly: accepting suggestions uncritically, believing in them passionately (and often perversely) and executing them slavishly, even automatically. So it is that anyone taking up a new craft or art may very easily hypnotize himself into doing the wrong thing—even against his will. To cite a familiar example: the person trying to learn to ride a bicycle will run right into a solitary post because, concentrating in fear on the image of what he should not do, he fixes his attention on it and, against his will, obeys its suggestion.

The fourth fact on which the military psychologist relies is, perhaps, rather a set of facts, which may be stated suc-

cinctly as follows: To assure the successful hypnotizing of an
enemy it is necessary for us to make him too weary or too
comfortable (mentally and physically) or too bewildered to
think straight and act resolutely. Then we can gain his un-
critical acceptance of a wrong course of action either directly
or indirectly. We gain it directly by awakening in him a passionate desire for an object, or by frightening him into believing that something must be done at once, or the object
will be lost—thus hurrying him into an anxious adoption of
the method for attaining it which we know to be fatal. We
gain our end indirectly by awakening the liking for the object
through associating it with a situation, person, thing, or
symbol (picture, for instance, or song) which he finds pleasant,
or by putting him through the process, without his being
aware of it, of giving his consent to a course of action, causing
him to say, as by slogans, for instance, that he likes something,
on the theory that it is hard for a person to reject something
of which he has gone through the motions of approving.

The fifth set of facts on which the military psychologist
relies is that a victim can be made to believe passionately in
or hold stubbornly to a course of action under these circumstances if the suggestions are made to him slyly, insinuatingly,
and yet forcefully; in such a way as never to jolt the will or the
judgment into action, while at the same time stimulating the
imagination and instinct. The suggestions must therefore be
made not too explicitly but strongly: they must be objective
and easy to understand, but not define—like a bit of panto-
mime. They must be given quietly and confidently, as if they
were obvious recommendations, quite sound. They can also
be insinuated, while the mind is concentrating on something
else. And they should be repeated frequently, but with enough
variation in external form to prevent the victim from noting

how repetitive they are and thereupon becoming suspicious of them.

Finally (sixth), the military psychologist relies on three ways of assuring that his victim will act wholeheartedly enough in carrying out a foolish plan to wreak his own destruction. These ways are: that of making him feel the desperate urgency of acting too fast, through lulling him into complacency and frightening him with the spectre of annihilation; that of enraging him, so that he acts blindly; and that of discouraging him, taking the heart out of him.

In all this, the military psychologist is merely making use of hypnosis as a weapon by assuring its six conditions, which are: 1) physical passivity; 2) immobility; 3) fixed attention; 4) mental passivity and submissiveness; 5) repetitive, objective suggestions; and 6) urgency. A subject is most easily and effectively deprived of his powers of deliberating rationally and of maintaining control over himself when he is taken willingly into a quiet, darkened room and put into a relaxed posture which he holds steadily while he submissively fixes his attention on one spot and receives quiet suggestions which he is urged to obey as soon as possible.

It is obvious that most of these conditions exist or can be made to exist in any war and in any battle. The expert assuring of them accounts, in fact, for much of what proved effective in Hitler's strategy and tactics: the war of nerves assuring physical passivity; the "sit-down" (Sitzkrieg) assuring immobility; the apparent attack on one point (France) assuring the fixed attention; the encouragement of belief in a false sense of security (the Maginot Line, the Munich "promises") assuring the mental passivity; the well-planned time-schedule of victories, one following the other with relentless, frightening, machine-like precision, as well as the continuous rumors by fifth columnists, both assuring the steady, repetitive objective suggestions; the suddenness and surprise of the attack through Holland and Belgium, as well as the startling new techniques, with their great speed, giving little chance to think, assuring the urgency. Perhaps the staggering effect of original sin in rendering man subject to deadly misdirection through hypnotic fascination is nowhere better illustrated than here.

But if it is best illustrated in military warfare, it is, unfortunately, almost equally well illustrated in non-military; that is, in economic, political, and ethical warfare, to say nothing of that in which Fate, as the pagan would say, alone would seem to be the enemy. Hypnotic fascination is practiced, alas, not only by generals, but by most of those who run our great industries or control our media of communication; by those who use salesmanship for the winning of the battle for profits and by those who use all forms of artistic and literary expression for winning the battle of ideologies.

We need only analyze the conditions of billboard, car-card, magazine, and radio advertising, to see that these are almost ideal for hypnosis, in that they catch their victims in conditions of physical and mental receptivity, convince by repetition rather than logic, and whip into unthinking action by instinctive and passionate incitement. Their effect, moreover, increases as their victims become more and more "conditioned" to the making of thoughtless decisions; in fact, it would be terrifying here in the United States (as the story of the Nazi tyranny, which made use of such means, well shows) were it not for the crudity and brashness with which the advertisers themselves, in the search of quick profits, over-praise and render suspect their products.

No less well-armed and skillful in the use of this technique of hypnosis than the generals and the commercialists are the ideologists; for they have at their almost exclusive command an instrument that could well have been devised by an expert hypnotist—the moving-pictures. All we need do is glance through the brief description of the conditions ideal for hypnosis and compare them with the conditions of the moving-picture theatre and of the pictures themselves to be (I hope) appalled at their congruence. From the darkness, the musical accompaniment, the very flickering of the central screen, on up to the single thematic point that is being made repetitively and objectively incident by incident and the emotional urgency by which the point is made—without the vaguest suspicion by most members of the audience that they are doing anything but enjoying an amusing story or a true picture of life—nothing, absolutely nothing, could be better designed for seduction than the moving-picture. As the Encyclical on the Cinema points out, this form of art is perilous in the extreme. The magazine does, to be sure, possess the advantage of persuading its readers by its stories to adopt and cherish principles of a way of life the means and methods of which the advertisements then persuade them to buy; and in this way literature works as the helper of commercialism and vice versa: one of them (I let the reader choose which) crouching behind the victim while the other gives him the final push. But for all that, the moving-picture is, single-handed, incomparably the most effective medium of persuasion of them all, as is shown by the astonishing number of magazines devoured by the movie-fans everywhere.

And bad as these means are, taken singly, they are infinitely worse taken in conjunction and considered as part of our heinous economic-social system today. Consider the full round of demoralization through which the usual factory worker goes day by day. Out of fear of want or economic and social degradation or because of a promise of luxury in his "free" time, he stands before a machine for eight hours, frequently knowing little about what it makes and caring less.

Thus softened, he is persuaded hypnotically by all kinds of advertisements, songs, magazines, and the like to try to achieve a state of arrested emotional development called romance by marrying a glamor girl who has been similarly persuaded to become one (and to become, incidentally, only that). These two frequent the "movies" together, where they are hypnotized into believing all the romantic nonsense—thoroughly anti-Christian—of the codes by which their favorite heroes and heroines "live." In these codes all truly Christian motives are simply ignored, the audience being thereby trained to solve all ethical problems without adverting once to a single spiritual precept, like a Beatitude. ("Where's your self-respect," "Is that the decent thing to do?" Never: "Where is your Charity?" "Is that true humility: where is your meekness?"). Here the inadequate and mortally specious codes of naturalism and humanism are alone suggested as acceptable, or even possible, Christian belief being made either ridiculous or merely sentimental and humanitarian (as in "Going My Way") or simply negligible enough to be ignored entirely, in the interests of "tolerance," which last form of treatment is as Cardinal Newman long ago pointed out, the most insidiously dangerous of all. If, as Baudelaire has said, the greatest triumph of the Devil is to have convinced mankind of his not existing, then he certainly seems to have found in the "movies" a marvelous instrument for making that triumph a lasting one. Our factory hand, therefore, and his soon-to-be-divorced glamor-girl wife—and theirs is, of course, no exceptional case—end by a loss of the very Faith without which it is practically impossible to see clearly what is wrong with the system in which they are caught: they are hypnotized into accepting the system which hypnotizes them to their own destruction.

What, then, can avail against the mystery of iniquity as

it is here considered; that is, as the source, not only of wrong moral decisions, but also as the source of a darkening of the soul, with its consequent disruption of technical habits? How are we to train our students so that they will be ready both in mind and in heart to resist Evil itself, to overcome it, and to follow whole-heartedly the promptings of the Holy Spirit?

First of all, we must open their eyes to the dangers about them, showing them clearly just what it is they are resisting and why they are resisting it. They must be brought to recognize that in commercialized civilization neither the ends proposed by the leaders of it nor the means employed to attain these ends have the necessary qualities of soundness, efficiency, and beauty, any more than the men concerned have the saintliness, the professional skill, and the heroism that is to be desired. We must show our students how the earthly paradises at which the people about them are aiming—the Leisure State, for example—would be, as Benson shows in his masterly novel, *Lord of the World*, nothing more than antiseptic, dehumanized hells. We must, moreover, be prepared to expose the means that are to be used in the attaining of these paradises, showing them to be what they are, immoral, ineffective, meretriciously glamorous: the hypnotic trickery of men ruled by lusts (for a "high standard of living") and fears (of competitors). We must show them the ugliness, indeed the frightfulness, of a system whereby one set of "interests" tries to reduce every other set to a brutish state of impulsiveness through robbing men of the full use of their critical powers and their free will, in the name of "salesmanship."

In all this, we must make our students, not merely know, but *feel*, how essentially evil are the forces with which they are confronted: not the men themselves, but the powers and

principalities of whom these poor men are the pawns. Charitably, unsentimentally, justly, we must be careful to point out
all that is good in the opposition: in their leaders, their
methods, their *esprit-de-corps*, their individual "soldiers" and
then go on, with no raising of the voice, no name-calling, no
smearing, no screeching, to show with the stark eloquence of
facts how dangerously even the well-intentioned and the brilliant have become enthralled by the Prince of Darkness, to
their ultimate bondage and destruction.

Especially must we avoid turning our students into the
dupes of their enemies through giving them, even tacitly, an
education in false hopes, an education in day-dreams that will
unfit them to deal with the realities of life. We must not permit them to fall prey to the opiate fantasies of what is called
optimism, lest when they are rudely shaken out of these, they
may be plunged into a paralyzing despair or into a bewilder-
ment that makes them easy victims. To tell young men and
young women (or even to let our silence suggest to them) that
they have the right to freedom from want, to freedom from
fear, to a high standard of living, to an advanced education and
to the luxuries which, so it seems, come in its train necessarily;
to "inspire them with the hope" that they may legitimately
expect—given sufficient good-will—to have a steady, well-pay-
ing job, a good home, an automobile, a radio, a healthy family,
secure old age, and so on; not to make them wisely aware of
the stupidity, the weakness, the ugliness, and the sinfulness
they may expect to discover, not only in others, but in themselves; not to prepare them for the irritations, the shocks, the
disgusts, the anxieties, the disappointments, the bitterness, of
life: all this is but to mistrain them, if it is not to do the work
of Satan himself, who could wish for no better aid. Let us not
send our soldiers into the battle under the impression that
they are going on a fairly comfortable expedition in search of

a Blue Bird. Or, to vary the figure: if we would keep them
from the bog, we must show them the ugliness both of it and
of the will-o'-the-wisp.

On the other hand, we ourselves must by personal example, by the ideal imaginative examples afforded us by the
Fine Arts, by instruments and surroundings through the
beauty of which shines forth the beauty of Christianity,
indeed by the persuasiveness of all the God-founded beauty
in the cosmos, make our students not only see, but rejoice
in the soundness, the rightness, the heroic gloriousness of
our divine cause, our divine leadership, our cleansed and sacramentalized means, our divinely established rewards of peace
and joy, even here on earth, our divinely assured worthiness
as persons in the image and likeness of God, redeemed by His
Only Son; our divinely established body, the Mystical Body
of Christ.

Here, we must make use of every legitimate means at our
disposal, to train the student, not only to resist demoralization, but also to act, at the very least, confidently, and, at best,
enthusiastically.

Of these purposes, we can best accomplish that of assuring in the student a proper state of confidence only if we
begin by analyzing to determine at least some of the principal
causes for his lack of confidence; after which, we can see,
fairly easily, what we are to avoid and what we are to do in
overcoming it.

To appreciate what we face here, let us consider for a
moment what the perfect education in discouragement would
be like—how it would be best achieved; for, in that way, we
can discern most clearly at least what must be avoided in a
sound education in Hope.

Now, if we were setting out to give a boy a thorough
education in discouragement, or despair, we should do so best,

I think, if we could make him feel certain in his heart of the following things: that it is unnatural for a human being to do anything well—especially, for him to use his higher faculties fruitfully and pleasantly; that only that thing which is done well (or which can be done well) is worth doing at all; that to do a special thing well (speak a foreign language fluently, for instance, or solve mathematical problems readily) requires a special talent; that whereas that football coach who impresses his men with his own knowledge, without making them feel that they can attain a level of skill at least the equal of his, is a very poor coach, the teacher is a "real authority" who impresses his students with his knowledge, while he suggests that they, of course, could never expect to attain anything like it. These and allied assumptions form an ideal basis for an education in discouragement.

They become doubly effective, of course, when the teacher himself holds them, or at least does nothing to suggest that he does not hold them. When he shows by the way in which he talks and acts, by the very way in which he gives out assignments, for instance, that he has forgotten that, although as fallen and perverse, man does not naturally use his higher faculties willingly and well, nevertheless, he does do so as being in the image and likeness of God, as redeemed by Christ, and as enlightened by the Holy Spirit—when the teacher becomes cynical through a failure to see this vital distinction, inevitably he infects his students with his sense of futility, aggravating their own. So, too, does he confirm them in a mild coma of hopelessness when he permits them to believe that he thinks education is a queer business, largely a matter of chance: a process in which information is presented to talented students who, if they had the will-power could get most of it for themselves, while the untalented students take "the stuff" down in the hope of being able to reproduce it in blue-books for the sake of a good mark—the whole effect being not so much to get persons ready to perform reasonable feats as to "train" somehow "the intellectual virtues." The teacher who thus assumes his students into an habitual state of hopelessness, is, as a master of the art of discouraging, worth his weight in atom-bombs.

Now, it must be clear that training in due confidence is based on attitudes and notions the very reverse of these. One of the most important arts of teaching, the art of encouraging, is mainly the art of raising the student to his highest state of development by "assuming him" into it; by never failing to show him that you consider it natural for him to master what he has set out to master. Obviously, a teacher cannot assume a student into an ability beyond his native endowments, his training, and his maturity; but we might do well never to forget that no teacher—expert in intelligence testing or not—can tell what a student can do (how resourceful he is and how philosophically he can think) until that student has been given a fair chance to show what he can do—the kind of chance which the professional, rather than the easily discouraged dilettante, always gives himself. A teacher who expects much will get more than he expects; a teacher who expects little, will get less.

Even if this fact were not clear from the way in which every society usually gets from its members what it expects of them (if it expects great poets, it usually gets great poets; if it expects great saints, it usually gets great saints)—even if this fact were not obvious, we still find evidence enough for it in education itself—in the education of athletes. Who does not know that once a record has been broken, almost anyone can break it after that; but that the record would not have been broken in the first place unless the champion had been assumed into breaking it?

Above all, however, we must see that unless we proceed by the method of wise and charitable assumption, we are liable to endanger the Hope, to say nothing of the Faith and Charity, both of our students and of ourselves; our actions may come to look strangely like the actions of those who believe that since men have emerged only recently from the ruck of primal matter, it is naive to consider them as perverse but essentially capable of God-like action—beings not only privileged, but endowed by God with the power, to cooperate with Him in the restoring of the world. Let it not be said of us that we crippled our students by not responding properly ourselves or by not teaching them to respond to the virtue of Hope.

Moreover, we shall do well to use all the resources of hypnotic fascination as described in this talk, *providing* that we use them legitimately; that is, that we capture the mind in order to lead it into thinking for itself; and that we quiet the will in order to redirect it and fire it with rational enthusiasm for the right object and with rational disgust for the wrong. Man needs to be captivated into enjoying truth and goodness and into acting in accordance with them quite as much as he needs to be captivated into accepting error and sin. It is for this reason that God made all things beautiful and beautiful each in its degree. Beauty is the divine lure and the divine reward.

And since all great art is designed to cast a spell in which the appreciator will be hypnotically induced to look on, enjoy, and be fired by the beauty of some one of the profound truths of God's creation, causing the appreciator not merely to know, but to *realize* it, then all fine art can properly be thought of as a form of captivation which delights the mind with the truth that sets free and makes ready the will for using that freedom wisely. Let us not forget that although the immediate pur-

pose of every great work of fine art is to entertain, its ultimate
and highest purpose is to take captive so as to free: to fascinate us into a responsiveness to the Gifts of the Holy Spirit
and spur us into a production of the Fruits. And it is our duty
as well as our privilege to aid it to fulfill its highest function.

As far as possible, indeed, we must make sure that we use
all beauty, the beauty in all things, in this sacramental way;
by everything he hears and sees, the student must be made to
delight in his Christian way of life. All things, from the statues
in the college chapel to the format of his textbooks must be
quietly eloquent of the rightness of that way.

Not that I would ask that his furnishings be elaborate or
luxurious. Certainly, they must not be pretty. Christianity is
beautiful, not pretty. Rather, his surroundings should be
worthy of men who may some day be martyrs. Think what
the effect on students' minds must be when they see about
them on all sides things which convince them that to be
Catholic is to be sweet, soft, willowy, foggy, hazy, effeminate,
pietistic, sentimental, perfervid, unsophisticated, provincial,
pretentious and tasteless. Then think of the effect on the
mind and heart of the West Pointer of everything with which
he comes into contact in his training: how subtly, unsentimentally, and soundly it makes him realize the greatness of
his cause and his vocation—how it makes him feel the sub-
limity of mud-covered heroism. If the vision of guarding the
city of man can be made thus appealing, how much more appealing should we not be able to make the vision of building
as well as guarding the City of God?

But this argument has been long and circuitous. May I
therefore conclude it by resuming its main points and adding
one or two concrete suggestions.

Sin, I have said, is the main enemy of skill; for the most
skillful action requires the cooperation of the powers of the

body and the mind, all working together in harmonious peace under the firm control of a grace-inspired will. It is only when men are free of fear and anger and the other passions, it is only when they have a delight in perfection and in the love of God and of their patrons out of love for God; it is only then that they can lose themselves in their work and produce the very best of which they are capable. But sin, original and actual, has made the peaceful cooperation of the faculties difficult; and malice has put the technique of hypnosis to the service of enslaving men to sin. The users of this technique employ it to fascinate their fellow men, victimizing them for the sake of profit or for the establishing of a so-called civilization in which pride and concupiscence will be the main motives, a civilization as second-rate as only vicious motives can make it. Our task, therefore, is to recognize these facts, unveil them in all their ugliness to our students, present to them the vision of the Kingdom of God on earth, train them to respond to this vision, awaken in them the confidence that God will be with them in their attempts to make it come true, and turn them into heroes of craftsmanship who do their share in making it come true.

I suggest, concretely, that the least we can do to this end is train our students to resist the blandishments of the enemy. We should establish true courses in Aesthetics in our colleges, courses in which our students are taught to discriminate between true beauty and glamor in all its forms, between the highest beauties and the lowest, between created beauties and Beauty Itself, God. These courses must be so conducted that students will come to respond to the higher beauty more intensely and happily than to the lower, so that they will find it difficult thereafter to prefer the image of a whited sepulchre to that of the blood-blackened Crucified. In every other course, moreover, we should see to it that every truth is duly appreciated not merely for itself and its own goodness and splendor, but for the goodness and splendor of God of which it is a refraction. Especially is this obligation laid upon those whose task it is to expound the moral virtues or to present dogmas of the sacred Mysteries of Christianity.

Further it would be well for us to recognize our courses in the Fine Arts, especially those in Literature, for what they are and deal with them accordingly. We must see them as courses in which students are trained to respond to the beauty of the truths of wisdom and to act on them habitually, almost subconsciously. We must therefore take careful heed that every work of art studied in these courses be analyzed to determine just how much wisdom it does contain; just how beautiful its truth really appears in the light of Christian Revelation; just how beautiful the artist presenting it would wish us to consider it, and how he would like us to act upon it; what persons, things, codes of conduct he wishes us to feel for and to feel against, and, in either case, how sentimentally; what codes he is slighting or causing us to disprize by not even mentioning them; to which of the virtues, from the theological on down, would it dispose us (or not); and which of the Fruits would it aid us to produce? Since every lie contains a grain of truth, to what extent can this or that work of art be used by us to help ourselves in the appreciating of that grain; how can even the anti-Christian production be thus made to subserve the interests of the Kingdom of God? All of which need not exclude consideration of the work on a lower level as an imaginatively pleasant recreation or an amazing technical achievement. Analyzing works of art as if they were minor expressions of inspiration (and they are liable to be more rather than less dangerous if they are not so analyzed) is only to be fair to them all, since it is only to judge them by their aims.

Finally, I would call attention to what Pope Pius XI said

(in his Encyclical on the Cinema) and urge that we do something more than analyze the mistakes of our enemies here— that we meet the well-presented Utopian dreams of heathendom with the even better presented vision of Christendom. That we answer novel with greater novel, play with greater play, moving-picture with greater moving-picture. It is high time that we establish professional graduate schools in the Fine Arts (and modify our college training in relation to them) which will assure to our graduates careers dedicated to the spreading of God's own propaganda, the Truth pure and simple, by a training as stiff as that of our medical schools or our law schools, so that the power of the fascination of Truth may be put to the forming of men and to the assuring of the conditions in which these men may serve God not only with charity, but with charity enhanced by skill.

XII

The Position of the Fine Arts

I~N~ THE present chapter, I shall attempt to do three things:—
first, I shall try to indicate how the fine arts are required by,
and may be integrated into, the general training of the Catholic student. Then I shall try to show how they themselves
make use of and integrate various kinds of knowledge provided
by other courses. And finally, I shall try to suggest what these
considerations imply for those who conduct such courses.

Thus, I will attempt to show how the various arts of drawing, painting, sculpture, stained-glass, architecture, singing,
etc., as well as those of English composition, rhetoric, creative
writing and literature, all fit into the training of the Christian
for his vocation as priest-prophet-maker-ruler. I will here attempt to show how even the acquisition of the fine arts in
their elementary form—for the purposes of direct, non-aesthetic communication—implies some reference to disciplines
like logic, psychology, ethics, the philosophy of craftsmanship,
religion; and then, how the acquisition or the appreciation of
these arts in what is usually their subtlest form—that which
has for its purpose an edifying entertainment—implies some
reference to these and to other subjects as well, including a
philosophy of beauty. Thereafter, I shall note what seem to
me some of the distinctions which we must keep in mind in
any effort to straighten out this subject of the fine arts.

Now, the fact that the fine arts, as these are commonly
understood, work naturally and easily into the four-fold vocation for which Catholic training is devised, becomes evident,

I think, as soon as we give them another name, the better to fit them into the full range of arts, so that we may see them, not simply as distinguished from manual arts, but as another group of the liberal arts. And that better name for these arts is the *communicative*.

For, calling them communicative enables us to see clearly the way in which they do help the student to fulfill his functions as priest, prophet, maker and ruler; this name enables us to focus on an important fact which otherwise we might overlook, the fact that there are two kinds of communicative art: one which is concerned with the primarily non-aesthetic and the other which is concerned with the primarily aesthetic form of communication. It enables us to see, in other words, the difference between the arts in which entertainment is secondary and those in which it is, in a sense, primary. We can then also see that even in the first of these two kinds, we should distinguish between that directed towards God and that directed towards man. For the problem of producing proper works of communication with God is primarily the problem not of suiting what we have to say to what He can understand, using the forms of expression with which He is familiar; it is, of course, that of learning how to free ourselves from the limitations of our own inarticulateness. In acts of worship, our main need is to pray as eloquently, as unconstrainedly, and wholeheartedly, as *fluently* as possible. For this purpose, we must have at least as much practice in fashioning the things needed—the prayers, chants, statues, vestments and the rest—as will enable us to make our own those with which the Church and its master-artists have traditionally provided us. Consequently, every student will do well to master the vocabulary and grammar of chanting, of sculpture, of stained-glass, of painting, of architecture, of the "properties" and the "staging" of the Mass. At the very least he should know these things well enough to construe understandingly not only the Latin of the Missal so that it becomes his own utterance, but also every sign, symbol, gesture, image, sound, movement and color before him, that they too may become, by *active adoption*, his own utterance. The *full* exercise of the function of priesthood implies, in fact, a thorough course in basic design.

The exercise of this function naturally implies also an appreciation of Him Who is served by it. It implies an appreciation of God as Beauty. To be a sound user of the technique of design, obviously the student must be moved with grateful love for God at the realization of how beautifully He has made all things and of how transcendantly beautiful is He Himself. For this purpose, if for no other, any course in the fine arts would have to be connected intimately with the course in philosophy of craftsmanship, with the one on the philosophy of beauty, and with one on the Mysteries of Christianity presented as beautiful. For if men who are trained to make things understandingly learn to admire and love their fellow craftsmen as makers, they also learn to feel an awe of God and to love Him as the *Factor Omnium*. And unless any work which the student performs is an admirable piece of craftsmanship, it is lacking in a certain honesty and splendor, so that it is not worthy of being offered to Him Who is Honesty, Rightness and Splendor. So, too, would every course in a fine art as required by the function of priesthood mean the connecting of its doctrines with the courses which provide it with the meanings to which the student was to respond and for which it was to afford him the means and the tone of expression; it must be connected with courses, that is, in the philosophy of beauty, as this would be understood by St. Augustine, and in the Mysteries of Christianity as these are presented by Scheeben.

The function of prophethood implies the bringing of

men to God in two ways: through one's work and through one's utterances, whether these latter be in stone, sound, pigment or written word. How the first of these things would be done, how it would be possible to bring men to God through the splendor of one's work, it is the task of the philosophy of craftsmanship to show, just as it would be the task of Ethics and Moral Theology to show how it is possible to bring them to God through the splendor of Christian courtesy. But the second way, the bringing of men to God by one's utterances, obviously implies that the student should be trained in the arts of explaining, teaching and persuading.

And here we see again how the fine arts draw upon the others, since the arts of explaining require properly that a student be given some training in Logic, Psychology, and the basic principles of Pedagogy. All these disciplines determine the arts of composing, or making up a diagram, or writing a simple piece of prose, or giving a simple lecture or even dispensing "the Catholic's ready answer." These things can be done really well only by the student who knows and has practiced, amongst others, such principles as those of classification, and definition, the laws of association of ideas, of over-learning, of going from the known to the unknown and from the more acceptable to the less acceptable. So too, the art of persuasion implies reference not only to the principles underlying explanation (and it certainly implies reference to these), but also to the psychology of attention, of emotion, of motivation, of cogitation, of deliberation, as well as to those principles of ethics which should govern the use of the means we now know of as salesmanship and propaganda.

Naturally, these arts of explaining and persuading are similarly required by the student if he is to fulfill his functions as maker and ruler, if he is to carry out his economic, political and social duties as a Christian in his community. There is no work which a student may take up at which he will not be required to instruct, or dispose himself to be instructed, nor any at which he will not need to persuade, or dispose himself to be duly persuaded. The arts of teaching men supernatural truth and persuading them to obey it differ very little in technique from the arts of teaching men natural truth and persuading them to act on it.

Thus far, we have been observing how the arts of communication which are not concerned with affording positive pleasure, but rather with saying things transparently, movingly, and excellently, how these arts are called for in the pattern of practical education that we have been considering; and we have also observed how they themselves cannot be properly taught or prosecuted without advertence to such disciplines as Logic, Psychology, Ethics, the Philosophy of Craftsmanship, the Philosophy of Beauty, and Theology, as well as to the study of what is called in art schools Design.

When we turn now to the arts which are concerned, as a first necessity, with the affording of an aesthetic experience, we see that these, too, can best be regarded as essentially forms of teaching—or, better still, perhaps, as forms of *coaching*. For the writers, the painters, the musicians, the sculptors, the architects, and the rest know that if the other artists of civilization—those who conduct our enterprises, our social organizations, our government—are to act wisely, either as individuals or as officers, in all the critical moments of their lives, they must do so in the proper state of body, mind, and soul. Great fine artists recognize the obvious truth that a successful act of any kind implies that the person performing it must have the energy, the information, the enlightenment, the skill, the virtue, and the morale necessary; and they try, as well as the art of each of them permits him to do so, to make sure that their fellow liberal artists will have all these things.

Let us consider in order, then, the various effects which the fine artists aim at in trying to assure these things, and observe what such effects imply: what they suggest he must know if he is to attain them properly—Christianly.

And, first, the effect of energizing. As everyone knows, unless a person has the energy required for a task, in no matter what field, he will not be able to accomplish that task. He will not be able to think straight. He will not be able to resist his foolish impulses or his passions. And he is liable to fall prey to all forms of slothful escapism. For these reasons, the great writer, the great painter, the great musician, and the rest, all realize that one of their tasks is that of providing true recreation—the re-creation that leaves their readers, their spectators, their audiences, refreshed mentally and physically—made ready for their next undertaking in life.

Not that any great artist is subject to the delusion that because he must be entertaining and recreative, he is accomplishing his highest purpose in so being. He knows the difference between a *sine qua non* and a *summum bonum*. Just as a good cook considers her work not that of tickling the palate, but that of nourishing while, and as a result of, tickling the palate; or a good physical trainer knows that his work is not simply that of providing the fun of games, but that of assuring the health of his charges while and through providing the fun of games; so Homer, Shakespeare, Mozart, Fra Angelico considered their work to be not that of merely entertaining, but that of edifying so entertainingly as not to seem to be edifying at all.

But even to be able to fulfill wisely the simplest function of entertaining well—even to know how to put a reader or an audience through a vacation that is a sound one, not one of escapism or wishful thinking or demoralizing imaginative luxury, the artist must have a firm grasp of certain principles drawn from at least three sciences. He must know the psychology of sentimentality, of day-dreaming, and of what is called the mechanism of compensation. He must know the moral theology of pleasure-seeking and of curiosity. And he must know enough about Pelagianism to see how it can appear in stories about "the better sort," "the regular guy" and Mrs. *Wiggs of the Cabbage Patch.*

The next function on our list, that of informing, is provided by art in the guise of vicarious experience. The historical novel or play, the historical picture or genre painting enable us to re-live the experiences of men of other times, other backgrounds, other places, as they faced situations not unlike our own. The story of a given locale or way of life does much the same thing as does a travelogue. So too, may the arts give us the "feel" of how men generally think and act, provide us with a fairly good descriptive knowledge of human nature and of destiny. Great art will often provide us with a descriptive science of life effectively because palatably. Moreover, it will train our very powers of perception: the great painter increases our ability to see what we are looking at, providing the new and fresh vision of a master perceiver; the great musician and the great poet tune our ears. In short, not only do the arts help us fill out the picture of what we have never seen. They also help us sharpen the vision of what we do see.

Clearly, the fulfilling of this function requires that the artist develop a keen sense of history and a sure understanding of the laws of observation, to say nothing of his knowledge of geography and sociology. He must come to a determination of just how valid is the picture of life given by fictive representation, just how valid it could be, how valid it is usually taken to be, and what can be done to guard against the invalid inferences which it may stimulate. He must know very exactly how secondary to poetic truth is the scientific truth in which it is embodied or by which it is illustrated.

The next higher function, that of enlightenment, consists of course not so much in descriptive as in causal explanation. By anything from cartoons to poetic dramas, the great artists can present crucial instances which bring out the universal truths of wisdom and cast light on the kinds of information which men have acquired either by direct experience or by the primarily informative sciences or arts. Just as the geometrician can present a hypothesis, a figure, and a systematic elucidation of it in proof of that hypothesis, so can the great artist present a situation, a plot, or even a musical idea as a hypothetical case and show how its inner logic "proves" a hypothesis in accordance with which one may learn to understand actual human life in terms of ideal human life. He can complete the lessons of historic truth with the lessons of poetic truth, or, better still, he can present the causal principles of life as interpretations of the descriptive ones. His is the casuistry of the probable and normative, rather than of the merely actual.

It is obvious that such an artist needs to know the principles of wisdom in accordance with which men should live in order to attain ultimate happiness, especially the principles of free will and Providence and of their interrelation. He must know the logic of demonstration by means of the single crucial instance which is a valid hypothetical case. Certainly he must know the difference between the exceptional instance, the average case, the dull crucial instance and the intensely engaging crucial instance. Naturally, he must be able to recognize these in every field in which his plot must be laid—economic, political, social, religious. And he must be on guard, himself, against the fallacies into which he is likely to fall, especially those of bias and propaganda.

Next, since energy, information, and even enlightenment are not sufficient for enabling the ordinary person to solve problems, however well they may enable him to recognize problems, the artist tries to choose situations which engage the cogitative sense—the inventiveness, the resourcefulness of his readers or of his audience. His hypothetical case is, when possible, a challenging one or is presented in a challenging way, like those of a Platonic dialogue. The dramatist and the the novelist, for instance (as we can easily see in detective stories) put their reader by means of choruses, or reflective interludes, or *confidants* through the equivalent of a Socratic dialogue.

For this purpose, of course, the artist must know the psychology of cogitation and of insight, as well as the philosophy of the way in which universals can be embodied in particular contingents. He must, in short, be a master of teaching by the case method.

The artist's concern with virtue is inevitable since the most universal truths leading to ultimate happiness are moral and religious: nothing done irreligiously being valid, anything done religiously being valid. His illustrations, stories, songs will at best be concerned, however indirectly, with negative or positive principles of asceticism. They will dispose us, intellectually at least, to the avoidance of sin, the embracing of virtues, the recognition of the need for correspondence with the theological virtues and the Gifts of the Holy Ghost in the production of the fruits. Thus, even a pagan writer like Homer shows, time after time, that the cleverness of Ulysses is not enough; that he must also exercise prudence, justice, fortitude and temperance, and that even these virtues are ineffective without the cooperation of divinity. Naturally, therefore, the great artist draws upon all the sciences of morality and shows how their principles are manifested in the conduct of life. In this way, he may be said to integrate everything from the sacramental principles of ascetic theology to the humanistic ones of ethics and of etiquette. Ideally, he makes use of that great and greatly neglected section of the *Summa* on the social virtues.

But, of course, not only must a work of art make its appreciator see or realize which truth he should follow, and which error he should shun, but it should make him do these things enthusiastically, inducing his heart and his head to cooperate happily. He should be made to like avoiding immoral actions and carrying out virtuous actions. In this sense, the fine arts are *the* morale builders for the Church Militant. By the charitable presentation of folly, they can awaken the compassion which restrains the observer from the committing of that folly; by the joyful presentation of heroism, they can awaken the admiration which induces the observer to imitate that heroism. By inciting the observer to feel the right emotion in the right intensity about the right thing, as these emotions should be felt in the principal affairs or situations of life, the sound artist can not only offset the bad training of the conscience given by the unsound, but he can also fortify all the good training given by any master of the liberal arts. Instead of conditioning his audience to a mere ill-organized, irrational code of feeling, based on self-respect and humanitarian pity—a kind of sentimental substitute for a conscience—he can make it easy for them to see clearly, and to abide enthusiastically by, the rational decisions which are based on the code of justice and charity. Through making them feel as well as know how much better it is to have a disorderly household with children than a neat apartment with a dog; or a family circle and happy laughter rather than cafe society and mordant

wit; or a happy marriage rather than an affair of courtly love
à la Hollywood; or obscurity in Christ rather than tabloid pub-
licity;—through making his audience feel rightly in such ways
as these, the fine artist (and his interpreter, the teacher of fine
arts) can assure their being disposed to the proper code of
courtesy, patriotism, piety and charity. He can enable them to
live in the emotional tenor befitting a Christian.

On the emotional training provided by the fine artist, indeed, may often depend the final value of all the other arts.
For of what avail is it to the student to know what he ought
to do and how he ought to do it, if he has no enthusiasm for
doing it, or if he is excited by the glamor of doing its opposite?
Unless a student is habituated to consenting to those ends
and those means to which he has learned to give an intellectual
assent, his whole training may be virtually nullified by the
counter-training provided by years of subjection to advertising, propaganda, moving-pictures and best-sellers.

By the same token, the teacher of the fine arts must know
enough about these matters to train students not to allow
themselves to be misled by the glamor of false and unwise art,
and to set themselves for a proper response to sound art. (Incidentally, I can think of no more useful course, at least for
many students, than one which would consist of weekly attendance at a popular movie or the reading of a best-seller as
selected by a moral theologian who was also a trained aestheti-
cian, to be followed by a general informal discussion and by
his final elucidation of the issues.[1] Certainly, it would be a
good thing if those who conduct our courses in ethics or moral
theology would draw their case material as much from fiction
as from either history or personal experience. For it is from

[1] Since writing this, I have been told that such a course is already being
given in a college in California and in The Catholic University of America.

fiction that students draw the lessons about life which they really believe.)

Now, there is at least one obvious objection which will have occurred to many of my readers as I have been going through this analysis of the so-called aesthetic arts—the objection that no artist could possibly think of all these things while he was turning out a work of art, and certainly he could have no complete scientific background of the kind that I have been suggesting. Indeed, some of the scientific principles here alluded to were not discovered until long after innumerable great works of art were produced. The answer to this objection is twofold: first of all, it is of course true that no one turning out a work of art consciously adverts while so doing to the principles governing it. On the other hand, unless he obeyed those principles without having to think about them at the time (because he had thought about them a great deal in previous practice periods) he would turn out a very poor work of art indeed. The man who thinks of the principles of riflery at the moment of shooting may well miss the target; the man who shoots in accordance with them by habit will hit the bull's-eye. Secondly, although these great artists did not possess an *explicit* or a *scientifically formulated* knowledge of moral theology, for instance, or of psychology, they did possess an implicit, first-hand understanding of these principles. As geniuses, they could appreciate the force of molecular truth long before men had enucleated it atomically.

I may also have given the impression that because the turning out of great works of art is difficult, and because it apparently requires a vast fund of knowledge, the turning out of merely acceptable works of art and the appreciating of the great works of art also prove difficult and also require a vast fund of knowledge. I may likewise have suggested that I expect students to aim at great skill both in the turning out and in the appreciating of all works of art. If I have done these things, I have done them unintentionally. All, it seems to me, that a Catholic college of liberal arts can expect to do here is to graduate students who have a firm grasp of the elementary principles of all the communicative arts, and an active appreciation of them which is the result of having tried their hands at them. In the essential arts of direct communication to God and to man, of course, they should be expected to acquire exceptional skill. In the others, they should be expected to gain a sound vocabulary and a feeling for the grammar and idiom, but not necessarily eloquence.

Now, the main problem facing an administrator here is that of getting rid of false notions concerning the purposes of the fine arts, and that of changing the methods of training to accord with the true notions of these purposes. It is for him to make others see, for instance, that non-aesthetic communication such as prayer or Gregorian chant is to be judged almost entirely by the excellence with which it does what it was *primarily* designed to do. Thus, since the primary form of the worship of the Church is, as the *Mediator Dei* carefully points out, liturgical worship, then the chant, the statues, the pictures in a church are to be judged by their suitability to that kind of worship first, and their suitability to any other kind secondarily, and their suitability to any other effect only very incidentally, if at all. Certainly, they are not to be appreciated in the same way in which they might, perhaps, be appreciated in a concert-hall, or in a museum. A piece of Gregorian for example, is not to be judged by how musically interesting is its structure, or by how *pleasantly* it makes those who are *listening* to it feel as *individuals*. It is to be judged by how well it enables a congregation *singing* to *pray* wholeheartedly thereby as *members* of the Mystical Body of Christ. And so for every other such instrumentality of expression: it is to be judged by its fulfillment of its main purpose.

Another false notion which must be destroyed is the assumption that we train best in the *craft* of communication through training in the *appreciation* of the fine art of it. The fact is, of course, that the craft of communication is one thing and the appreciation of the fine art of it is another. By the mere fact that he is a human being (as the most primitive of peoples show) anyone can be taught the grammar of design, the "languages" of painting, singing, choric reading, speaking, lettering, drawing, sewing, etc. And these languages are valuable, in fact vital, even though the acquisition of them does not of itself turn students into Dantes, Fra Angelicos or rivals of Solesmes. To follow the method of asking the students to turn out poetic masterpieces before they have learned the prose idiom of paint or sound or pen or brush is simply to confuse and discourage. It does not help the student who might one day become that rare thing, a great artist, and it is no less discouraging to the ordinary student. This method is indeed almost as confusing and discouraging as would be that of a teacher of mathematics who asked a boy to appreciate the theory of relativity while he was still struggling with elementary algebra.

Perhaps the greatest difficulty which faces the administrator who wishes to reform courses in fine art is that of getting teachers to appreciate the necessity of giving to appreciation of the art the second place and to practice of the craft the first place. We have been so long taken in by Epicureanism that it is extremely difficult for us to realize that appreciation results from craftsmanship, not craftsmanship from appreciation. If it is true that the best way of learning a language is to go where you need to speak it and then speak it, perfecting your grammar as you go along and acquiring your taste for its literature almost by absorption, so it is true of every other art of communicating that you will become an expert appreciator of it and of the full range of its masterpieces best by learning its language natively, that is through using it yourself.

It is only, then, when the fine arts are seen to be the arts of communication, and when their full importance and complexity is appreciated as aiding man to fulfill his vocation as priest, prophet, maker and ruler, that they can be properly mastered and will be properly integrated with all the other arts.

XIII

The Principle of Integration[1]
—a Key and a Résumé

THAT education is ideal which is integrated so as to meet the requirements of Christian practicality.

Even without any special training in pedagogy, we might be led to this belief merely as a result of putting together certain well-known truths of natural and revealed theology and by working out carefully their full implications. We should grow fairly certain, I think, that the phrase, "Christian practicality," gives us the key to education as we reflected on the following chain of propositions:—God is Pure Act. God is Love. A creature is most itself in expressing the God-like qualities in which it participates. Man is in the image and likeness of God. Man is most himself, therefore, when he is *acting*, and acting in the spirit of Divine Love. Man can best act in this spirit of Love when he is acting as a member of Christ's Mystical Body, whose spirit is the Spirit of Love. Without doubt, then, that education is best which trains students to be most truly active (most practical) and most truly loving (most Christian).

All of which means, a little more concretely—as we have

[1] That the principle of integration proposed in this chapter is arrived at by something more than mere wishful thinking is proved, I believe, by Christopher Dawson when he shows that some such principle as this is necessary for maintenance of any culture and that, in fact, it was this principle, or one indistinguishable from it, which men followed in producing Western Culture itself. See his *Religion and Culture* (Sheed & Ward, 1948) Chapter X, and his *Religion and the Rise of Western Culture* (Sheed & Ward, 1950) Chapters II and III especially.

seen now more than once—that every perfectly educated person should naturally be expected to solve skillfully the problems and perform skillfully the tasks of priest (at least those of the lay priesthood), prophet (spokesman), maker, and ruler. Ideally, before he is given specialistic training, he will be liberally and thoroughly trained in the arts essential to the skillful prosecution of these tasks as they occur in either lay or priestly vocations. And because his primary necessity and highest aim are to live, as a member of the Mystical Body, a Christ-life in terms of his own, the student must obviously master, or strive to master, all the purely spiritual and the temporal arts which such an incarnational life supposes.

In the abstract, then, Christian practicality, when logically analyzed, would seem to be an unexcelled principle of integration.

But is it so in fact?

There is perhaps no better way of answering this question than by our starting with what would appear to be an extremely narrow interpretation of this principle and seeing where it would lead us. What kind of education would be required simply for making a student into as good a Catholic as possible? And how much narrower would such an education be than any we now have in our Catholic or our non-Catholic American colleges? Or that we might hope to have? For, if we answer these questions logically, we shall attain, I believe, a very clear notion of the ideal principle of integration and some insight into what we must do in reforming our instruction in accordance with it.

Let us consider, then, what might happen if a group of men who were expert Catholics in every sense of the word—men who were actively carrying out, with great skill, what the Encyclicals preach—if such a group were to band together to spend, as master artists in their fields, some of their time in training apprentices to be nothing more or less than good Catholics like themselves.

In the nature of things, they would, of course, concern themselves primarily with two general ends: first, the art of worshipping God as this has been set forth in such Encyclicals as the *Miserentissimus Redemptor*, the *Mystici Corporis*, and above all, the *Mediator Dei*; and, second, the art of executing the Catholic program of social reform as this program has been outlined in all the various Encyclicals and allocutions concerned with it, from the *Rerum Novarum* on, those on Education and on the Cinema included.

Obviously, a training for mastery of the arts of worshipping would have to ensure, first of all, a course in active participation in the Mass: a course in which, as we have seen, the students would be shown as quickly as possible how to join with their fellow-worshippers in offering the Mass through the hands of the priest as alert members of the lay priesthood. Meanwhile, they would be given, perhaps by means of homilies at the Daily Mass, season by season, clear non-technical explanations of the significance of each phase of the Liturgical Year, so that they might thus live that phase intelligently and fruitfully.

At the same time also, the students would be taking courses in Church Latin and Gregorian chant, as well as studying the Messianic tradition as this appears in both the Old and the New Testaments. (As soon as possible, they should be given some training in the Dialogue Mass—largely, I think, to get them anxious to begin to master the art of singing the Mass.)

The next objective might well be that of showing the students the arts of confessing, communicating, praying the Divine Office, using sacramentals, meditating (especially on the Collect of the Day), saying the Rosary, making retreats, and getting the greatest fruit out of all forms of Devotions. This particular objective would include training in appreciation of the nature of Baptism and Confirmation, and of how to correspond, in the spirit of recollection, with the life and grace received in these Sacraments. It would also include preparation for the possible reception of the sacraments of Holy Orders or of Matrimony, as well as of Extreme Unction.

Now, if the masters in Christian living who are constructing this course of study went on to provide some training in the various fine arts directly concerned with the worship of God—sculpture, painting, stained-glass, architecture, lettering and illuminating, silversmithy or goldsmithy, the designing and making of vestments, etc.—the curriculum, even at this point, would contain: a course in participation in the Mass, a course in the art of worshipping adeptly throughout the Liturgical Year; a course in the Messianic tradition; a course in receiving the sacraments, in praying and in devotional practices; one in Latin; one in Gregorian chant; and one in iconography and in "trying out at" what are unhappily called "liturgical" arts.

Even so, it is clear that all this training would still be inadequate; it would still enable the students to be no more than fair experts at the functions of the lay-priesthood in its narrowest sense. Nor would it enable them to fulfill these functions as artistically as possible. To do that, they would need sound courses in Dogmatic Theology and in Philosophy. For a truly artistic performance of any task demands, as master artists would certainly realize, a technique that is based on scientific and philosophic principles. No students would be true masters of an art if they performed it in accordance with mere rules of thumb. Especially would they not be true masters of the art of worshipping; since this is an art the full understanding of which requires sound training in both "theologizing" and philosophizing. To gain some grasp of the Mysteries of the Uncreated, to read the vestiges of the Trinity that are to be found in all things, to proceed from creature-hood to Creator by way of negative transcendence, everyone must acquire some skill in dealing with the problems of Cosmology, Psychology, Ontology and Theology. Otherwise, he would have only an imaginative, not a profoundly imaginative-intellectual concept of God and His relationship to His creatures. Nor would he sufficiently deepen and rectify his knowledge of God and His Mysteries unless he proceeded from a knowledge of the truths of faith to some deep appreciation, however imperfect, of how they are so and why they are so.

Moreover, students cannot acquire a sound knowledge of philosophy and sound habits of philosophizing and of theologizing, unless they base this knowledge and these habits on a sound knowledge of the descriptive and causal sciences of the main orders of being, mineral, vegetable, animal and human; thus, at the very least, on sound knowledge and sound habits of dealing with matters physical, chemical, biological and psychological.

Nor could they expect their habits of thinking scientifically and philosophically to be sound until they had mastered the fundamental habits of logical thinking, experimentation and measurement: until they knew both Logic and Scientific Method, and the Philosophy of Quantity, Mathematics.

So, then, if the masters of the art of Christian living who are constructing our course of study want simply to train students as scientifically and philosophically grounded artists in the art of worshipping, they must add to their curriculum studies in the basic principles of Logic, Physics, Chemistry, Biology, Experimental and Speculative Psychology, Cosmology, Ontology, and Theology.

Next, if these masters were to consider training their students for their Christian function of prophet or spokesman, they would see that this function requires primarily skill in the various arts of fictional and non-fictional writing and speaking—and in the appreciating of the works of the masters who provide us with both examples of wisdom and models of expression. At the very least, therefore, the proposed college should provide courses in writing and in Literature and in Aesthetics—courses that would prove adequate for these purposes. Ideally, such a literary training should also include a course in general Linguistics and in the Greek and the Latin necessary for the appreciation of the fountain of all eloquence —the Scriptures and the Fathers—especially as these same disciplines would also unlock the doors to the treasury of philosophy and literature, modern as well as ancient.

Now, such an education as this so far outlined could hardly be called—even from the point of view of the world— very limited in its curriculum: many an Oxford man has had to be content with far less.

But, from a Catholic point of view, this education would still be gravely defective, since it would offer no training in social works: in bringing all things, economic, political and sociological, to a head in Christ. It would do little to show students how to make civilization, how to conduct it, and how to sacramentalize it. To this end, there would be required a course in the philosophy of skillful making—a course in what might be called General Technology—the philosophic principles governing all forms of making; as there would also need to be courses in Moral Theology, in the techniques of Catholic Action, and in the norms of courtesy:[2] courses which would give basic principles governing all the typical conditions of social life and authority. As a minimum, then, if the curricu-

[2] As these are worked out, for instance, in the *Summa Theologica*, 2^a—$2,^{ae}$ Qu. 101-122.

lum we are considering is to train students for their Christian functions as makers and rulers, as well as those of priest and prophet, it would call for courses in General Technology, Economics, Politics, History, Moral Theology and Sociology (especially that of Catholic Action).

Now, if we examine carefully the education that is here proposed, can we not honestly say that it is far broader, rather than far narrower, than any now proposed by non-Catholics? I think so. For if it be objected that what would be given in such an education would be (1) a mere smattering of (2) narrow because "slanted" instruction; the answer to the first objection is that no true master of any art could ever be content with so unsound and unscientific an equipment as is afforded by a mere "smattering," and we are presuming that the teachers of this course of study would be true masters of the arts of Christian living. And the second objection can easily be answered, since the man with a truly Catholic mind, faced with the problems of the real world and inspired with the desire for discovering, in the spirit of real Scholasticism, the "grain of truth in every lie" is hardly likely to be less comprehensive and objective than are his opponents who give matters an irreligious slant. It is true that those who are interested primarily and almost exclusively in Apologetics might be likely to "slant" the teaching of Cosmology, Epistemology and Psychology. But it is equally true that those who are interested in training students to be something more than apologists and "examples of devotion," who intend to train students to become scientific and heroic priest-prophet-maker-rulers—would never be permitted, by the very fullness and realism of their objectives, to acquire a one-sided biased view of things or to encourage others to do so. Real artists learn very quickly from life never to misprize the sciences on which their skill depends or to underrate the value of pure science, for itself and for the foundation it gives to applied science.

So far, we have considered the outlines of a curriculum whose principle of integration is Christian practicality. If now, we ask what would be the general view of education naturally adopted by those who would devise such a scheme, we can answer that it might best be described as, in the best sense, "military." Masters of Christian living setting out to train young men and women would be interested in giving every student an apprenticeship that is also a cadetship. They would feel obliged to give him a systematic rehearsal in meeting the crises of life—preparing him to win the inevitable battles for the peace of Christ in the reign of Christ.

Therefore they would consider their task to be that of enabling every student to work out, in every field, an intelligent estimate of the situation in which mankind finds itself at all times, and at the present day; they would show him how to gain a clear understanding of the obstacles to be met, of the enemies inner and outer to be overcome, of favorable forces and conditions, of possible methods of attack and of plans for sound campaigns. They would aid the student thus to outline the general and personal problems to be overcome, to select the most important, and to determine which of these he should be able to solve by the end of each course and of the whole four years' training. Then they would arrange practice periods for the acquirement of this or that skill and this or that combination of skills as these are called for in the solving of the problems (which would be made, throughout the four years, increasingly harder, larger and subtler).

Naturally, these problems would be limited in number and kind; for several reasons: first, it takes time to develop any habit of skillful action; second, although all problems should be real, concrete and particular, they are a waste of time if they are merely peculiar and ephemeral, they must be concrete but *typical*; not just this problem and then that, but an *instance* of this kind of problem which naturally leads into and aids in the solution of an *instance* of that kind of problem. They should, in other words, form a "case-system," similar to, but superior to that used today in many law-schools.

Thus, to give an example or so, a student taking up the course on participation in the Mass might well be asked, first off, what he thought was the ideal way of "going to Mass" and be required to give a full impromptu answer to this question. Next, he might be required to read the *Mediator Dei* and asked to revise his "theory" in the light of this Encyclical. Thereupon, he could be required, with some guidance, to work out an "estimate of the situation" for himself, his fellow-students, his own parish and the Church: to determine what the spread between the actual and the ideal is. Then he should be encouraged to work out what ought to be done (prudently and charitably, of course) to lessen that spread; specifically, what he himself must do to master the art of corporate worship and to help others to do so.

Or again, when the student takes up Economics, he should be put through a similar training: being asked to tell what he thinks is wrong with our economic situation, to check his opinion by the *Rerum Novarum* and the *Quadragesimo Anno*, to make up plans for remedying the situation in accordance with the objectives and guiding principles of these works, to check these plans by those set forth by the Distributists, the Cooperativists and the proponents of the Industry Council method (the Bishops of the United States), as well as those set forth by anti-Christian or agnostic economists. (Of course, the working-out of problems such as those given in these two examples would run concurrently with the whole course in question.)

Ideally, the teachers, as practicing artists in each field, would be able to give the kinds of guidance, set the kinds of problems, and raise the kinds of theoretical issues which, because they are crucial, would evoke the keenest interest. They could, in fact, set real problems which the students knew and felt to be real—any answers to which, even the guesses of students, would be at least indirectly or negatively helpful; with the result that students could realize that they were, even in their mere practice periods or most tentative essays, making some contribution to the furthering of Christendom. They could feel from the outset that they were not undergoing a mere series of drills, but a true, realistic, valuable apprenticeship, differing from that of carpenter or plumber, lawyer or doctor, only in being concerned with more primary problems than are these fellow-craftsmen.

The use of such a "case-system" in each course would give the education we are considering the value of integration in terms of Christian practicality in act, as well as in theory. And it would, I think, be quite possible to gain concurrently here the value of another method of integration, the integration of a variety of forms of skill as this is induced by focussing on one or other of the main institutions of mankind. In the Freshman year, for example, the students might well be required to turn out a thesis on the Church: in the Sophomore Year, one on the Home; in the Junior year, one on the Business House and one on the School; and in the Senior Year, one on the State—each to call for as full and deep a correlation of various branches of knowledge and skill as could be achieved.

These major theses should be, I suggest, the work of *teams* of about seven students each, who, under the guidance of a teacher (which guidance would be less and less from year to year) would learn how to work out a useful and crucial thesis, how to analyze it, how to trace out its minor hypotheses, how to investigate and test each of these, how to formulate valid conclusions, and how to devise plans based on them. Students could thus be taught how to cooperate on a scientific investigation under the guidance of a master artist: how to integrate knowledge and skill socially. (Something like this is already being done in the superb year-books put out by the students of Marygrove College, Detroit.)

Finally, every student should, I believe, be required to make out, very early in his college career, a tentative, general plan of life, one which he would be called on to revise periodically throughout his course: a plan that would encourage him to prepare for living a unified life; hence one which would enable him to evaluate and correlate all the forms of knowledge and skill which he was acquiring, so that he would appreciate them not only for themselves but also as related to his vocation and place in the world—what needs to be done by everyone in general and by himself in particular being indicated to him with progressive clarity by his study of the Encyclicals, by his growing knowledge of himself and his powers, by the light God gives him in response to his prayers as to God's special will for him.

We have now discussed the curriculum and the general view of education, with its consequences, of a college whose principle of integration is that of Christian practicality, established by masters in the arts of Christian living. Now, what about the manner and methods of teaching in such an institution?

A college conducted by such practicing masters—artists in residence—would undoubtedly make use of all methods of instruction, with those of coaching setting the norm: as far as possible tutoring being considered ideal, then laboratory, workshop and seminar, and last, class-room recitations. Lectures would be, of course, essential; but they would be regarded more as means for epitomizing, codifying, and systematizing information needed or already acquired than as first sources of information. The proportions of trial-and-error experimentation to memorizing; of practicing to notetaking; of imaginative application to examination-taking; of conferring, discussing and analyzing to attending lectures;—all would resemble very closely the proportions maintained in modern athletic coaching. The pedagogy of art would never be sacrificed to the pedagogy of science: the methods for developing skill would never be ignored in favor of "covering the ground."

Another great advantage of this Church Militant view of Integration is that it also enables us to integrate the extra-classroom activities with those of the classroom. It enables us to correlate the activities of the Student Council, the Debating, Literary, Dramatic and Musical Clubs; the Sodalities, the Catholic Action and the N.F.C.C.S. groups, with the work in class-room, laboratory, seminar or workshop. For if the regular instruction is determined primarily by the requirements of the campaigns for the restoration and redemption of society as these are implied by the Encyclicals, so must the activities of these various student organizations be considered to be the immediate putting into effect of the principles studied in class for the implementation of the Encyclicals. These activities would be to regular instruction what games are to "skull practice" and field practice in football. They would become part of the educational process, rather than something thought of as apart from that process. And they would constitute such valuable interneship—such valuable training in facing realities and incarnating ideals—that they could be included as integral parts of the instruction, each student being required to have taken part, by the time he graduates, in one form of each of these kinds of activities.

Moreover, what is true of these collegiate activities is also true of all part-time and summer job activities: these can easily be made the first real testing-ground—what military men call the baptism of fire: they can be used as the bridge between preparation for living and full living.

Not, of course, that in all this, the intellectual training itself is to be neglected. After all, the virtue of art is, as some of us seem to forget, an intellectual virtue. If art is not to be developed simply by "reading up" on the conditions and principles governing an activity (no one becomes a Sophocles simply by memorizing the "Poetics" or another Aristotle simply by memorizing books of logic); neither is it developed by unscientific practice. If we are to deal with things intelligently, ourselves included, we must know them in their causes, in their primary as well as their secondary causes—indeed, in their ultimate and primary Cause. And if one is to know these causal principles as well as they should be known, one must be able to appreciate them as individually true, good and beautiful and as collectively part of a cosmic metaphysical system. Consequently, every teacher, in explaining the doctrines of the science of his liberal art, must be careful to make clear the compass and degree of certitude of these doctrines (their truth); he must indicate their utilitarian and ethical implications (their practical and ethical goodness), and must bring out for contemplation the intrinsic and the symbolic beauty of their truth and their goodness. The teacher who does no more than tell the facts of his science teaches not even two-thirds of it. For, in addition, he must make clear the interconnections of the particular doctrine he is teaching with the doctrines of other fields and levels of knowledge. He must find its *loci* in the whole realm of truth.

Now, whether everyone may consider the various kinds of integration proposed in this talk to be ideal or not, we all can agree, I feel sure, that the correlation of otherwise departmentalized knowledge is wholly desirable in any college. Moreover, this is a form of integration that we can begin to work towards immediately with very little change of our present ways. For every faculty could certainly form within a short time a Committee of Correlation made up of at least one representative from each department, all to gather around a table at frequent intervals to explore the interrelationships of their various sciences, so that these interrelationships might become increasingly clearer and easier to indicate to students when the separate doctrines are mentioned in various classes.

Suppose, for example, at the meeting of such a Committee, the teacher of Chemistry were to explain, as he came to it in going through the basic doctrines of his science, the subject of "substance." After he had told what the Chemist's definition of substance is, the Cosmologist could be called on for a comparison of that view with his; the Biologist for a statement of the sense in which an animal is a substance; the Psychologist for a statement of the sense in which man is an individual substance of a rational nature; the Theologian for an explanation of the value of the concept of the virtual existence of elements in a compound as an analogy for making clear (or not) the Hypostatic Union, or for helping us to understand a little better the doctrine of Transubstantiation.

In some such way as this—I do not present this example as ideal—all the main doctrines of each of the various subjects could be taken up so that when any one of them was dealt with, all the others to which it was related in any way could be re-emphasized and connected with it by cross-reference. Even if each of our colleges went through only one subject a year in this way, we should soon have an enormous body of such inter-relationships to refer to both in text-books and in teaching. Ideally, of course, such a commission as this should be part of an institute of integration that would deal with the whole problem; but until such an institute does get established, at least we can all try for something of the kind in our own colleges.

That the education I have been describing meets the requirements laid down by a sound definition of integration is, I believe, undeniable. For, in general, integration may be said to mean the harmonious cooperation of forces resulting in well-coordinated actions which lead to the attainment of hierarchically ordered ends. And the education I have sketched certainly leads to harmonious cooperation of forces, since the principal remedy for the disharmony that was caused primarily by sin is sanctification; and the next most important means of assuring the harmonious exercise of faculties is their coordination through exercise together in the performance of tasks for which they were designed: the tasks given to men as heroic priest-prophet-maker-rulers in attaining the hierarchically ordered ends of establishing, conducting, sacramentalizing and offering sacrificially to God, the Christ, under the guidance of the Holy Spirit, civilization itself, for the building up of the Mystical Body of Christ and re-establishing all things in Him.

Now, whether all educators subscribe to everything that has been set forth in the course of this chapter or not, they can all, either as teachers or as administrators, do something towards carrying out whatever of this program seems to them worthwhile; and they can do so, I believe, somewhat more easily than would appear possible at first sight.

For one thing, they can hope that our Elementary and High Schools will soon be relieving them of the necessity for paying regard, in college training, to some of the more general and preliminary aspects of this problem—especially in the field of religion—as teachers on these levels come to see the task of education much as it is seen here. Then, too, they have most, if not all, of the necessary means for carrying out this program already available, in courses and equipment, if not always in textbooks and in teacher-training.

Thus, any teacher could easily make some change, however slight, in his or her course to fit it into the campaign of the Church Militant, even after the briefest of studies of the appropriate Encyclicals and Allocutions (and what a wealth of these, especially of the Allocutions, we usually leave untouched!). So, students entering our institutions could easily be given at least a brief orientation course in the ultimate purposes of their education; and this view could be further clarified, sharpened, and deepened by all the means already available—by Sodalities, Catholic Action groups, etc., as well as by the courses of study. Then, again, students could be encouraged in writing theses and holding discussions about subjects involving several sciences and philosophy and theology, thus learning to integrate otherwise uncorrelated disciplines. Finally, they could easily be given more practical guidance in the integration of their extra-classroom activities with their courses and with their future life work.

Put into practice *gradually*, then, all these suggestions will, I believe, prove feasible. What is mainly needed is the willingness to put them into practice, a willingness based on the recognition of Christian practicality as the integrating principle of education.

XIV

The Check-up

THAT this book may prove of some practical value to all its
readers, I venture to conclude it with a brief list of questions
that may be used as a check-up. May they act as criteria for
those who believe in the theory here presented and as a fruitful source of provocation for those who do not.

(1) *As to pupils:* Are we turning out quiz-kids, boy
orators, and model gentlemen—or young saint-artist-heroes?
Is it safe to leave them alone in an examination room, without
a proctor? Are they more expert at receiving and appreciating
than at achieving and serving? Is self-improvement or charity
first in their minds; have they at least the self-lessness of a
military school?

(2) *As to the school as a whole:* Is it a place of Christian
peace and leisure, where Christian masters coach and "bring
along" their Christian apprentices Charitably, training them
for responsible living? Or is it a place of "pressure," of hurry,
where wisdom has to be bootlegged because of rules, tests, reports, red-tape, activities, and the teacher's fear of not "covering the ground."

(3) *As for the curriculum:* Is it so proportioned that the
Mass actually is the central and primary, the all-important
event of the day; that the arts of religious living—participating
actively in dialogue and sung Masses, in the Feasts and seasons
of the Church; participating intelligently in the reception
of the Sacraments and sacramentals; performing acts of Christian courtesy and so on—are given their due importance? Is

the school ancillary to the Church's own method of teaching, or is it detrimental to it?

(4) *As to teachers:* Do we give over the teaching of religion to our best teachers—since this is the most important of all subjects—or to our mediocrities? Are our teachers judged by the habits of Christian skillful living shown by their students, or by the number of degrees from Protestant institutions they can point to? Finally, are they leaders, or are they merely drill-sergeants?

These, I submit, are vital questions; I submit them in all charity, because I believe that it is only when these and similar questions can be answered favorably that we can feel sure that our institutions are what they ought to be. It is only when our schools are primarily concerned with turning out, not cultured young men and women with minds well stocked with scientific information and philosophic apologetics, but young saints-in-the-making with the scientific skill needed for worshipping as members of Christ's Mystical Body, and for restoring all things in Him—it is only then that they shall be wholly worthy of the name Catholic. And when even a few of them do begin to be worthy of that name, they will dazzle us with the splendor of what they promise for mankind. For they will give promise of a civilization that will enrapture by its beauty: one in which no longer will the works of the flesh be manifest, "which are, fornication, uncleanness, immodesty, luxury, idolatry, witchcraft, enmities, contentions, emulations, wraths, quarrels, dissensions, sects, envies, murders, drunkenness, revellings, and such like" but rather one in which will be manifest the fruit of the Spirit: "charity, joy, peace, patience, benignity, goodness, longanimity, mildness, faith, modesty, continence, chastity." In a civilization of this kind, men will be truly educated, for they will "live in the Spirit and also walk in the Spirit."

Appendices

Appendix A

IT IS not often that a great educational institution has the courage and the wisdom to commission a large corps of scholarly investigators to make an honest, unsparing diagnosis of its defects and to offer a prescription for remedying them. The first reaction to the press report on the 267 page survey entitled, "General Education in a Free Society," issued after two years of careful study by a learned Harvard committee, is, therefore, one of gratitude. For such a report will undoubtedly have many desirable effects. First of all, even if it were not valuable in itself, as unquestionably it is, it would still serve as a remarkably useful indicator of what we must expect in education during at least the next quarter century. Next, it will undoubtedly also help to rid our education (once and for all, let us hope) of selfish dilettante-ism and selfish specialism, as well as of the men and methods that fostered these. Finally, it will make far easier than ever before the task of Rectors, Deans, and Professors in Catholic colleges to make these institutions as Catholic as they would like to make them.

It can be said that the report enables us to foresee, at least dimly, the next development in college and pre-college education because Harvard is an institution the influence of which on higher education in America it would be almost impossible to over-estimate. A great many of our colleges and preparatory schools are what they are either because they follow closely the lead given by Harvard or because they almost automatically turn away from that lead. As goes Harvard so

---

[1] Article written for *The Boston Pilot*.

go many of the colleges who depend upon it for staffing their faculties with Ph.D.'s. Then, too, many preparatory schools are designed to turn out prospective Harvard men. And these schools also affect, indirectly, other preparatory schools, serving somewhat as models for those that feed, for example, into Yale, Princeton, Williams, or Amherst. The report itself, moreover, suggests very frankly that it might be well for all preparatory schools, private or not, to arrange their courses with at least one eye on the revised Harvard curriculum (taking care to stress, for instance, study of a good factual course in American History). On the other hand, the course of development to be followed by those institutions which simply rebel against Harvardian theories should be fairly clear and predictable; for the ideas presented in the report are positive and clear enough (one might almost say dogmatic enough) to lead to a reaction equally positive and clear.

But whatever the value of the report as a means of foreseeing the next trend in American education, it certainly should have great value as a death blow to self-centered specialism and dilettante-ism. Under the system of free electives, teachers naturally assumed that young men who took their courses were intending to become specialists (probably Ph.D.'s); hence, the courses were composed and taught on this assumption. The later modification of the system, to one of concentration and distribution, prevented absolute narrowness or willful dissipation of interest; but the courses were still to be given as if every student of a given field were to be a Ph.D. in that field. Moreover, the student was encouraged to believe that he was acquiring knowledge, not in relation to other human beings, but only for his own needs— especially to become a "success" in a world of hard-bitten competitors. The report, however, makes it quite clear that in neither subject-matter nor methods of instruction will the merely self-centered student find any satisfaction from now on. Every student at Harvard hereafter is to be shown his relationship to his fellow Americans (and his fellow Europeans), as well as trained to deal with them patriotically and cooperatively. The curriculum and the methods of teaching are to be determined by the need for turning out high-minded citizens. Thus, the core of the curriculum is to be a certain group of required courses which will presumably make the student appreciate the fact that he lives in a certain culture and a certain place, with obligations to both. These courses comprise: one in The Great Texts of Literature; one in American Democracy, which would acquaint students with the problems with which they will have to cope as Americans; and another in Human Relations, apparently designed to make the sciences into at least part-time handmaidens of society rather than let them continue as unconcerned goddesses in ivory towers. The instruction also is to be humanized and generalized; instructors are to have smaller classes; and the opportunity of consulting tutor-specialists is to be limited to those students who are capable of making sound use of specialized knowledge. In short, Harvard is to turn out not self-centered go-getters or scientific, and philosophic escapists, but well-rounded citizens: Americans who are aware of one another's traditions and willing to cooperate and serve patriotically.

Now, in one way, all this is very good. It must surely help all American colleges to deal with that plaguey person, the materialistic parent who wants "his son to have the luxuries which he, himself, never had." To this kind of parent, college has long meant simply a place where his son could be given a chance to get the diploma, make the social contacts, acquire the polish, win the athletic fame which make success in the business world fairly easy. The college has been considered an institution for stuffing the mind with the "knowledge" that "is power"—the knowledge that will enable the student to gain a livelihood as "a big shot" in the business world, a vote-getter, a "clever" lawyer, or a well-paid professor. The fact that in the process his son might not ever become a decent citizen, to say nothing of a gentleman, or that he might lose his soul or let it waste away from lack of the Bread of Heaven, seemed not to occur to this type of solicitous parent. Having accepted, innocently and forgivably enough, the aims of our "leading" colleges, he naturally assumed that all other colleges—Catholic included—were to be judged by whether they had these aims and could attain them. Hence, the deans of all our colleges, Catholic and non-Catholic alike, have long been plagued by the demands of those parents who wished to have their sons transformed into materialistic saints—into "boys who would never do anything wrong"—except, of course, underpay the help; evict unfortunate tenants; take a little honest graft, now and then—or give it; drive a competitor out of business; run a gossip column; master legal chicanery, etc.

Now, with the publication of this report, we may have the glimmering of a new dawn. If its suggestions are adopted far and wide—and let us hope they will be—the moment may well come when deans will be able to say to student and parent alike: "No; your choice does not lie between an Arts college which trains you for selfishness and one which does not; your choice lies only between one which trains you for one kind of unselfish life and another which trains you for another kind of unselfish life."

When that moment comes, the deans of our Catholic colleges will be free to add: "Yes; it is all right patriotically to give to Caesar the things that are Caesar's; but it would also seem necessary to give to God something besides a few hours of study to the part men's ideas of Him played in building up the institutions of Western civilization. And that reduces your choice essentially to two kinds of college: one whose aim is to turn out men who are primarily patriots; the other whose aim is to turn out men who are primarily saints. Neither is likely to attain these aims fully. The question therefore simply is, which would you rather be trained at: a college whose motto reads, 'Seek ye first to be intelligent citizens—a sound people of a sound country—and all these things will be added unto you'; or one whose motto is, 'Seek ye first the Kingdom of God and His justice, and all these things will be added unto you'? You are not to be a Christian to win success; but, on the word of Our Lord Himself, if you are a Christian, you cannot but be, in every real sense, a success."

So it may well be that this report issued by Harvard will make doubly easy the task of all those Rectors, Deans, and Professors of Catholic colleges who are earnestly striving to reform these and make them as Catholic as possible. For it may well show parents and students that none of the leading colleges will any longer cater to the bourgeois, the epicurean, or the philistine; that they are *all* striving to get their students to lead some sort of dedicated life; and hence that the choice lies, as always, between a dedication primarily to Caesar or primarily to Christ. Then, it being granted that the curriculum of a Catholic college should be integrated in terms of this second aim, the authorities can go ahead rearranging that curriculum and the teaching methods in some such way as I have suggested in *The Idea of a Catholic College*. And perhaps we shall then see the day in which every Catholic college will whole-heartedly and undistractedly concentrate on training its students, to quote that book, "how best, in Charity, to participate in the Mass, to receive the sacraments, to make use of the sacramentals, to pray (liturgically as well as privately) to contemplate, appreciate, study, and work. Developing the natural faculties of its students to the utmost—their imaginations, intellects, and wills—it will promote all those sound habits of craftsmanship and industry, of economic, political, and social cooperation, of scientific investigation, of discrimination, and of philosophic and theological contemplation that will aid them, as members of the Mystical Body of Christ, to regain the integrity lost at the Fall, to sanctify themselves, to sacramentalize the world and society, while making a living (whether as professional men, business men, or craftsmen) and to share at all times as intimately as possible in the work of the Trinity, now and forever."

Appendix B

AN OATH FOR CATHOLIC COLLEGE STUDENTS

THE following is suggested as the kind of oath, similar to that taken by the medical or the military student, which might be taken by the Freshman class shortly after entering college and, with slight modifications, by the Senior class at Commencement. Its full implications could also be explained during orientation weeks or retreats.

O Almighty and All-loving God, You to Whose generosity we owe our very being; Who sent Your Only Son that by the merits of His selfless Sacrifice we might be not only redeemed, but raised to the dignity of membership in His Mystical Body and empowered to be, in His Name, under the guidance of the Holy Spirit, members of a royal priesthood, spokesmen of the Good News He came to announce, and co-workers with Him in the redeeming of the world;

Grant us, we pray, the grace and the strength to become the dedicated priest-prophet-maker-rulers which, no matter what our diverse ways of life, we are all called to be, in and through Your Son. Let us learn (continue to learn) to be one in the whole-hearted joining of our self-oblation with that of Your Son, Our Lord, in His Holy Sacrifice; so that, renewed thereby, we may go forth to live, not our lives by means of His, but His life by means of ours.

Let us learn (continue to learn) the splendor of Your inexhaustible Mysteries, that as prophets, spokesmen of their glorious truth, we may draw others to their light and joy.

Grant that we may acquire each new truth, first, for what

it tells us of You and for what it enables us to accomplish in clothing the naked, feeding the hungry, sheltering the homeless, bringing peace to the embittered and disconsolate, and Life to the sick of soul.

Let us in nothing seek our own advantage; never striving in any way to overreach our neighbors in business; nor prizing for what they are not the rewards of this world: the wealth, the pleasures, or the praise of men.

All that we are, every truth we shall learn (have learned) every skill we shall acquire (have acquired)—as all are from You, so all we offer back to You in Your service. Guide us that we may learn (continue to learn) to use them selflessly, in the Spirit of Him into Whom we have been incorporated; that each of us in his chosen work may possess the joy of sharing in establishment of Your Kingdom: the Kingdom of Truth and Life; the Kingdom of Sanctity and Grace; the Kingdom of Justice, Love, and Peace. Through Our Lord, Jesus Christ, Who with You, in the unity of the Holy Spirit, lives and reigns, God, world without end, AMEN.

Appendix C

CONTRASTING THEORIES OF EDUCATION

Non-Catholic	*Catholic*
1) The student is an individual,	1) The student is a creature,
2) capable of appreciating higher values	2) in the image and likeness of God and restless for Him
3) with weak powers each needing its special training	3) his faculties rendered uncooperative by sin
4) capable of developing sound habits of moral action	4) capable of being restored by grace, through the Redemption, to a state of supernatural life.
5) designed primarily for appreciating	5) designed primarily for acting
6) receptively (profitably)	6) givingly (Charitably)
7) hence to be taught	7) hence to be trained
8) for achievements: for getting ahead, making advances	8) for deeds and feats
9) in self-reliant, Epicurean, humanitarianism	9) of Christian heroism
10) in defending freedom and raising the standard of living of all	10) in sacramentalizing, in Christ, nature and civilization
11) by aiding in the spread of Democracy and all humane liberal organizations	11) by aiding in the growth and work of the Mystical Body as the leaven of the cosmos
12) through courses	12) through an apprenticeship
13) given by lecturers, tutors and examiners	13) under leader-coaches
14) in the scientific subjects that are the common heritage of the cultured	14) in the crafts and arts of making and sacramentalizing civilization
15) the main powers cultivated being those of observation, memory and analytic reason	15) the main powers cultivated being those of cogitation, resourcefulness, and synthetic reason (intellectual intuition)
16) the main virtues being enterprise, courage, self-reliance,	16) the main virtues being Charity, Faith, Hope, and the cardinal

Non-Catholic	*Catholic*
poise, tact, sophistication, fairness, tolerance, cooperativeness, generosity	virtues as subordinate to the Gifts of the Holy Ghost
17) the main "content" of education being the memorized intellectual knowledge of facts and principles.	17) the main "content" of education being realizations of vital truths of wisdom.

The Catholic believes that these views are not essentially contradictory: the true values of non-Catholic education are automatically taken care of, subsumed, by a truly Catholic education, in accordance with Our Lord's promise: "Seek ye first the Kingdom of God and His justice, and all these things shall be added unto you."

Appendix D

THE CHRISTIAN TEACHING OF SCIENCE

To RAISE the question, is there such a thing as a Christian way of teaching science, is to raise what is undoubtedly one of the most crucial questions in education today. It is to confront us, in fact, with what many educators today consider to be a real and serious dilemma. For, on the one hand, Pope Pius XI tells us, in the Encyclical on the Christian Education of Youth, that all our subjects must be permeated with Christianity; and, on the other hand, scientific theorists tell us that of its very nature science is neither Christian nor non-Christian, and that the very attempt to "permeate" it with Christianity is itself unscientific, it being contrary to scientific method to take into account any but purely rational, rather than religious, axioms and hypotheses in dealing with physical matter.

Clearly, then, the Catholic teacher of physical science, unless he sees that he is here facing no true dilemma, but only an apparent one, cannot help asking himself with some uneasiness how he can obey the requirements of educating both Christianly and non-Christianly at once. So, too, must a teacher of a social science feel concerned over this problem; for if it cannot be shown how the physical sciences can be taught as permeated with Christianity, he may well begin to question whether the social sciences have any right, if they also are to deserve their names as sciences, to be taught as so permeated. Obversely, if it can be shown that even the physical sciences can be taught Christianly *to their benefit as sciences*, then clearly the social sciences, as being concerned with choices made by the soul possessed of free will, have even more right to be taught Christianly.

Are we faced, then, with a real or a false dilemma here? And is it simply contradictory to speak of the *Christian* teaching of *physical science*?

That this dilemma is a false one, and that it is not in the least contradictory to speak of the Christian teaching of physical science, this being in truth the ideal way of teaching it—these are facts which become very clear, I think, as soon as we examine the suppositions underlying the non-Christian teaching of science and compare them with those underlying the Christian. It then becomes undeniable that the Christian method subsumes the non-Christian, including it and perfecting it.

For the non-Christian method of teaching science is based on the following suppositions:—

1) The main reason why a student takes up a given science is to acquire knowledge of it, by means of which knowledge he will be enabled to know and love the truth for its own sake, to become better acquainted with the world about him, to converse about it interestingly and appreciatively, to advance the frontiers of knowledge, and to get ahead in some business or profession.

2) This knowledge, which is first hand and accurate, is concerned with phenomena and the secondary causes of them. A scientist can no more be expected to delve into the ultimate causes of the phenomena with which he has to deal than a time-keeper can be expected to master Aristotle's definition of time. Science is primarily a positivistic and pragmatic business, not a philosophic one; and if scientific results and methods prove incompatible with common sense and philosophy, so much the worse for common sense and philosophy, which, as Relativity shows, are not strictly the scientist's con-

cern. Problems raised by these conflicts are outside his field; and it is very dangerous for a scientist to go outside his field.

3) Moreover, even if the scientist could legitimately spend time on such problems, the teacher of science could not: the time allotted to him is too precious for anything like that. For practical reasons, it is necessary, if the student is to be equipped with a well-rounded knowledge of a given science, that he be enabled to cover the ground of that science in a relatively short time: one year being given to the fundamentals of the science as a whole and about one year to each of several courses in the fundamentals of this or that special division of the science. Consequently, there is time only for the studying (or should one say the memorizing?) of the contents of lectures and textbooks and the gaining of some familiarity with the discoveries mentioned in these through the following out of instruction sheets and the suggestions of laboratory manuals, in such a way as to re-stage and observe certain classic experiments. The student is to be tested mainly by his ability to state the facts and principles of the science in written examinations and by the amount, accuracy and neatness of his work in the laboratory.

4) Naturally, no course in science can be entirely free of digressions, which will be of three kinds: that of showing the student the practical application in this or that business or profession of the more important doctrines of the course; that of pointing out occasionally the connection of a particular doctrine with some doctrine in a closely allied field; and that of warning the student against misunderstanding the moral or religious implications of a doctrine: showing him, for instance, that this or that doctrine does not lend support, as at first it seems to do, to this or that popular theory (like that of Birth Control or of Evolution); that it was perfectly possible for Pasteur and others to be great scientists and good

Catholics; that, from a strictly scientific point of view, Galileo was presumptuous; and so on. These digressions are to be indulged in sparingly, however, for two very good reasons: a science course is, after all, a course in science; and there is always so much to be mastered that there is seldom any time for extras.

These, then, are the suppositions in accordance with which a great many science courses are being conducted to-day; to many, perhaps to most, teachers they seem, in fact, to be the only legitimate suppositions. There is, however, another way of teaching science, a way based on the following suppositions:—

1) The main reason why any student takes up any subject, even a subject like Physics, is to learn to know God, to love Him, and to serve Him, whole-heartedly, and to know, love, and serve his neighbor for love of God—the ability to do these things being increased through the acquisition of wisdom, knowledge, and skill.

The student is to acquire wisdom, knowledge, and skill so as not only to became well acquainted with the world about him, but also to deepen his knowledge of the whole cosmos (earth, hell, purgatory, and Heaven) and of its Creator as His nature is indicated by His handiwork. It may be granted that he is to acquire knowledge for its own sake,[1] but he is to acquire it also and principally for the sake of the Gifts of the Holy Ghost to which it is ancillary (Wisdom, Understanding,

---

[1] I say it may be granted, because philosophically and theologically there is, it seems to me, some question as to whether we can really "love the truth for its own sake" as these words are generally understood. For, when we speak of "the truth" in this way, we mean either the Truth—that is, God as knowable—or the truth as a transcendental. In either case, we love it for its splendor; and unless I am mistaken, the splendor of truth is beauty; so that here we are, in fact, loving beauty, or loving truth for the sake of beauty. Moreover, the question may also be raised whether, in loving any one of the beauties of creatures, we are not really loving, however unconsciously, the Beauty of the Creator.

Knowledge, Counsel, etc.) and for the Fruits it enables him to produce (charity, joy, peace, patience, etc.). His training is to enable him to serve God and mankind effectively through leading a truly expert life, a life of professional excellence, no matter what his work may turn out to be. Naturally, it will enable him to converse interestingly and appreciatively; but, more than that, it will enable him to meditate, contemplate, and pray far better than he could otherwise.

2) The knowledge to be acquired in a science course is primarily skill: the student is to be trained first of all as an apprentice-scientist. Through hard, self-reliant practice, he is to learn how to observe, classify, hypothesize, experiment, measure, define, formulate, discern implications and invent applications, all in accordance with the principles common to all scientific methods and peculiar to the method of the given science. He is to learn to do these things, as far as possible, on his own, his memory being considered secondary to his cogitative sense, or, as Newman would put it, to his "illative sense." He is thus to acquire a fixed habit of using scientific methods in discovering and applying truths, wherever such methods are valid.

The information which the student acquires in a science course is to be presented to him simply as all the truth about the reality with which he is dealing that has thus far been arrived at by men studying a limited aspect of that reality by a method which is a refinement on that of common sense.

And although it is dangerous for a scientist, as a scientist, to go outside his field, if doing so means applying the methods of one field illegitimately to the data of another, it is dangerous for a *teacher* of science *not* to go outside his field and correlate it with other fields. For example: the student who has a clear notion of chemical substance can for that very reason be more easily taught the nature of personality than can the student who does not; and the teacher who fails to correlate such notions through fear of going outside his field is simply a poor teacher.

3) Above all, no teacher of science, or of anything else for that matter, can rightly permit a student to feel that Truth is not one: that common sense truth about matter is one thing, whereas scientific truth about matter is another and essentially different thing; that poetic truth is different from either, as is philosophic; and that religious truth has little or nothing to do with any of them. These truths do, of course, differ; and even knowing all of them about any one thing is not knowing *the* Truth about it as God knows it; but to give the faintest sanction to the student's feeling that they are radically different and irreconcilable, is, in effect, diabolical. Even at the cost, therefore, of not covering all the minutiae of a science, the teacher should always be willing to take time for helping the student to unify his knowledge and to transform it into wisdom.

Moreover, since one of the primary objectives of a science course is the development of scientific skills, a course should be considered a success as a liberal arts course when it has developed these, whether the student has "covered the ground" or not—although there is little reason to suppose that the student who has acquired these skills will not also have acquired as much factual knowledge as the student who goes in for memorizing. Properly, then, a scientific student is to be tested on his ability to observe, classify, experiment, and so on: if during the last six weeks of the course, he shows that he can do these things well, he is to be considered a good student.

4) Moreover, since the primary *general* object of the course is to enable the student to acquire as much wisdom as possible—that is, to increase his ability to appreciate

ultimate truths and act in accordance with them habitually, so as to live as God wills him to—it is not to be considered in any sense a digression when he is shown the philosophic and religious implication of every truth he masters: when he is shown, for instance, how Chemistry bears out the Aristotelian notion of substance and affords us an analogy for the Hypostatic Union; how Mathematics gives us some hint of the virtual simplicity of God; how Biology enables us to appreciate the fallacies of individualism, or the beauty of the Mystical Body of Christ; how Psychology enables us, under the guidance of St. Augustine, to acquire a better analogical apprehension of the Trinity; and so on. The student is to be shown how the methods of interpreting a text can also be applied to creation, the Book of God: being aided to see how a Bonaventure would deal with scientific truth, not merely for its literal, but also for its allegorical, moral, and anagogical significances. The student is, in fact, to be shown the most Charitable use, in contemplation as well as in action, to which he can put his knowledge.

These "digressions" should not, of course, be fulsome: they must be proportioned to both the student's need of them and to the truths on which they are based. A course in Biology, for example, is not to be made a course in the biological facts of interest to theologians or philosophers only; but neither is it to be made a course in which the impression is given that Biology and Theology have little or nothing to do with each other. If a pound of Theology to a tenth of an ounce of Physics is disproportionate, so is a pound of Physics to a tenth of an ounce of Theology: neither of these is the recipe for the proper nourishing of the young scientist as "the whole man."

If, then, the first of the methods here described is the typically non-Catholic and the second is the fully Catholic, it

Appendix E

BIBLIOGRAPHIES

1. Bibliography for the Chapter on "Secularism"

St. Thomas, Summa Theologica: secunda secundae, qq. 166 and 167.

St. Bonaventure's De Reductione Artium ad Theologiam. A dissertation by Sister Emma Therese Healy, St. Bonaventure's College, St. Bonaventure, N. Y. (1940).

"Collationes de Septem Donis Spiritus Sancti," Vol. V. S. Bonaventurae Opera Omnia; especially from last sentence of section 2 up to section 13 of Collatio IV.

The Philosophy of St. Bonaventure, by Etienne Gilson (Sheed and Ward), Ch. 2; especially from page 109 to end.

A Great Sacrament, by Dom Albert Hammenstede, O.S.B.; pamphlet pub. by Pio Decimo Press, St. Louis. (Pages 9-10 especially.)

"Liturgy and the Cultural Problem," by von Hildebrand; "The College Graduate in Parochial Liturgical Life," by Hayne; articles in The National Liturgical Week (1941), pub. by the Benedictine Liturgical Conference, 528 High St., Newark, N. J.

"Liturgy and Religious Education"; article by Rev. Ralph Kelley in National Liturgical Week (1944), pub. by The Liturgical Conference, Inc., 605 North Michigan Boulevard, Chicago, Ill. Also, the works he cites in his footnotes.

The series of articles, variously entitled, on liturgical education in practice, by H. B., in Orate Fratres, Vol. XVI, Nos. 1-7, 10, 11.

"Towards a Theology for the Layman"; article by John Courtney Murray, S.J., in Theological Studies, Vol. V., No. 3, Sept. 1944, pp. 340-376.

"Sacred vs. Secular Culture"; article by Graham Carey in *The Catholic Art Quarterly*, Vol. VII, Pentecost Number, 1944; Published by Cath. Art Ass'n, St. John's Univ., Collegeville, Minn.

"Living to Work"; article by His Excellency Archbishop Richard J. Cushing, D.D., in *The Catholic Art Quarterly*, Easter, 1945, Vol. VIII, No. 2.

Mater Ecclesia, magazine, Vol. 3, No. 3, Autumn 1945, pp. 70-71 and p. 77. Also, Vol. III. No. 4, Winter, 1945, article, "Theirs to Sing and Live," p. 109.

General Education in a Free Society; Report of the Harvard Committee, Harvard Univ. Press, Cambridge, Mass.

A Guildsman's Interpretation of History, by A. J. Penty (Sheed & Ward).

Five Great Encyclicals. The Paulist Press, N. Y. Following sections of "The Christian Education of Youth": pp. 52-53, section entitled True Harmony; p. 54, section entitled The Subject of Education; p. 59, section entitled Educational Environment; p. 60, section entitled The Catholic School.

The Encyclical *Mystici Corporis*, pub. by NCWC., p. 8, paragraph 10.

2. Bibliography for the Chapter on "Education and Catholicity"

The Encyclicals on:
The Christian Education of Youth
The Mystical Body (Mystici Corporis)
Christ the King

Diekmann, Godfrey, O.S.B., "Lay Participation in the Liturgy of the Church," in *Pius X, a Symposium*, published by the Conf. of Christian Doctrine.

Donnelly, Philip, S.J., "The Doctrine of the Vatican Council on the End of Creation," in *Theological Studies*, Vol. IV, No. 1., March 1943; and "The Ultimate Purpose of Creation according to St. Thomas," in *Theological Studies*, vol. 2, No. 1, 1941.

Healy, Sr. Mary, *St. Bonaventure's De Reductione Artium ad Theologiam*, St. Bonaventure College. Passim.

Scheeben, *The Mysteries of Christianity*, Chapters: VII (and its appendices); VIII; IX; XI (sections 44, 45, 46); XII; XIV; XV; XVI; XIX.

Weller, *The Roman Ritual*: The Blessings (Bruce, 1947), (Introduction).

Winzen, Damasus, O.S.B., "Anointed with the Spirit," in *Orate Fratres*, June and July 1946 (Vol. XX, Nos. 8 and 9).

3. Bibliography for the Chapter on "The Mastering of a Liberal Art"

Newman, John Henry, Cardinal, *The Grammar of Assent*, section, "The Illative Sense."

St. Thomas, *Sum. Theol.* I, Quaest. CXVII, Art. 1. and LXXVII, Art. 4.

Péghaire, Jules, *The Modern Schoolman* for Mar. 1943 and May 1943, article: "The Cogitative Sense."

Woodbury & Perkins, *The Art of Seeing* (Scribner's), *passim*.

4. Bibliography for the Chapter on "Sin as the Enemy of Skill"

Eltinge, Leroy, *The Psychology of War* (Revised Edition), pp. 1-113. Army Service Schools Press, Fort Leavenworth, 1918.

Eymieu, Antonin, *Le gouvernement de soi-meme*, Vol. I. (Perrin et Cie. Paris).

Jersild and Thomas, art. "The Influence of Adrenal Extract on Behavior and Mental Efficiency," from the *American Journal of Psychology*, July 1931, Vol. XLIII, pp. 447-456.

Pius XI, Encyclical on the Cinema.